AF600648

# THE RESTRAINT OF THE EXERCISE OF ONE'S RIGHTS

This dissertation was approved by the Reverend Bernard F. Deutsch, J.C.D., I.C.D., as Director, and by the Right Reverend Clement V. Bastnagel, J.C.D., and Doctor Stephan G. Kuttner, J.C.D., S.J.D., as Readers.

THE CATHOLIC UNIVERSITY OF AMERICA
CANON LAW STUDIES
No. 432

# The Restraint of the Exercise of One's Rights

A DISSERTATION

SUBMITTED TO THE FACULTY OF THE SCHOOL OF CANON LAW OF THE CATHOLIC UNIVERSITY OF AMERICA IN PARTIAL FULFILLMENT OF THE REQUIREMENTS FOR THE DEGREE OF DOCTOR OF CANON LAW

BY THE
REVEREND JOHN C. CALHOUN, A.B., S.T.B., J.C.L.
PRIEST OF THE DIOCESE OF BROOKLYN

THE CATHOLIC UNIVERSITY OF AMERICA PRESS
WASHINGTON, D. C.
1965

NIHIL OBSTAT:

REV. BERNARDUS F. DEUTSCH, J.C.D., I.C.D.
*Censor Deputatus*

IMPRIMATUR:

BRYAN JOSEPHUS MCENTEGART, D.D., LL.D.
*Episcopus Bruklyniensis*

Bruklyni, die xxi maji, 1965



MURRAY AND HEISTER, INC.
WASHINGTON, D. C.

PRINTED BY
TIMES AND NEWS PUBLISHING CO.
GETTYSBURG, PA., U. S. A.

TABLE OF CONTENTS

TABLE OF CONTENTS (Continued)

# PART TWO

## Canonical Commentary

TABLE OF CONTENTS (Continued)

Respectfully Dedicated

*with*

Reverence and Gratitude

*to*

HIS EXCELLENCY
BRYAN J. McENTEGART, D.D., LL.D.

*Bishop of Brooklyn*

# FOREWORD

The Catholic Church is a juridic society. Its members, by virtue of their baptism, are endowed with a theological personality (the infusion of sanctifying grace in the soul, the theological gifts and virtues, and the adoptive filiation to the God-head), and enjoy a juridic capacity (as a subject of rights and obligations) in the Church. It is by means of this juridic capacity that the members of the Church come to be the subjects of rights and obligations in Canon Law.

The object of this thesis is a consideration of the subjective rights of members of the Church, the exercise of those rights, and the restraints which are placed upon the exercise of those rights by the law of the Church for the benefit of the common good.

The right of private property will be considered as one which has been subject to legal restraint in its exercise. The thesis, therefore, will develop a fourfold historical conspectus of the restraint of the exercise of one's right of property. The first chapter deals with Roman Law and the institute of servitudes or easements. The second chapter considers feudal law and the contract of vassalage or enfeoffment. The third chapter sets forth the mediaeval notion of private property, the ownership of church property, and the law of alienation of church property which effectively restrained the right of disposition of church property. The fourth chapter is devoted to a study of the law of alienation after the Council of Trent, and also to a consideration of the source of the formula of canon 19 in the present Code of Canon Law, which deals specifically with the restraint of the exercise of one's rights.

The canonical commentary commences in the fifth chapter with an analysis of the theological and philosophical foundations of freedom and the restraint of freedom as contained in the law of the Catholic Church. The sixth chapter is concerned first with the subject of the legal restraint of the exercise of one's rights and secondly with the object of such a legal restraint. The seventh and final chapter draws several illustrations of the legal restraint of the exercise of one's rights from the Code of Canon Law.

The writer wishes to express his profound gratitude to His Excellency, the Most Reverend Bryan J. McEntegart, D.D., LL.D., Bishop of Brooklyn, for the opportunity of undertaking and completing graduate studies in Canon Law at the Catholic University of America and for his kind generosity in making this publication possible. The writer also wishes to express his gratitude to the Reverend Bernard F. Deutsch, J.C.D., I.C.D., who directed the writing of this dissertation, for his patient guidance and constructive suggestions in the preparation of the text. Similar gratitude is due to the Right Reverend Clement V. Bastnagel, S.T.L., J.U.D., Dean of the School of Canon Law, Catholic University of America, and Professor Stefan G. Kuttner, J.U.D., S.J.D., J.C.D., LL.D., Professor of Canon Law at the Catholic University of America, who served as readers of this dissertation and provided the writer with many thoughtful and scholarly corrections of the original manuscript. To the many others who assisted in the preparation of this dissertation the writer is sincerely grateful.

# INTRODUCTION

The restraint of the exercise of one's rights is not a simple idea; it involves several concepts. First, there is the concept of right, especially a subjective right. Second, there is the concept of the exercise of a right as distinguishable from the existence of the right. Third, there is that particular limitation of the exercise of a right which is a legal restraint. This legal restraint differs from a physical or moral impossibility on the part of the subject to exercise his right. It is also different from a legal prohibition, which does not involve rights at all but rather delimits human activity as, for example, the law which forbids the reception of Holy Communion more than once on any given day.[1]

The restraint of the exercise of one's rights as it is found in Western legal thought had its beginnings in Roman Law, and extended to many areas of law. It affected one's ability to enter into contracts,[2] even the contract of marriage,[3] to will property,[4] to inherit,[5] as well as to own property, whether personal or real.

---

[1] Canon 857: "Nemini liceat sanctissimam Eucharistiam recipere, qui eam eadem die iam receperit, . . ." Codex Iuris Canonici Pii X Pontificis Maximi iussu digestus Benedicti Papae XV auctoritate promulgatus, Praefatione, Fontium Annotatione et Indice Analysico-Alphobetico ab Emo Petro Card. Gasparri Auctus (Romae: Typis Polyglottis Vaticanis, 1917; Reimpressio, 1934).

[2] Henry F. Jolowicz, *Historical Introduction to the Study of Roman Law* (2. ed., Cambridge: The University Press, 1954), p. 58 (hereafter cited as Jolowicz).

[3] Jolowicz, p. 244.

[4] Fritz Schulz, *Classical Roman Law* (Oxford: The University Press, 1954), p. 205.

[5] "Feminae ad haereditates legitimas ultra consanguineas successiones non admittuntur . . ."—*Digesta* (4.8) 20: *Corpus Iuris Civilis,* 3 vols., Vol. I, *Institutiones,* quae recognovit P. Krueger; *Digesta,* quae recognovit T. Mommsen et retractavit P. Krueger, ed. stereotypa 15.; Vol. II, *Codex Iustinianus,* quem recognovit et retractavit P. Krueger, ed. stereotypa 10.; Vol. III, *Novellae Constitutiones, ed. stereotypa* 5., a R. Schoell; opus Schoellii morte interceptum absolvit G. Kroll (Berolini: apud Weidmannos, 1928-1929), I (hereafter the *Digesta* will be cited as D., the *Codex* as C., and the *Novellae Constitutiones* as Nov.).

# PART ONE

## Historical Synopsis

# CHAPTER I

## The Right of Ownership in Roman Law

The purpose of this chapter is to determine the origin and growth of the institute of property ownership as an expression of the restriction of the exercise of one's rights during the period of Roman Law.

### SECTION I. THE RIGHT OF OWNERSHIP BEFORE THE TIME OF THE TWELVE TABLES

Roman history before the time of the *Twelve Tables* (451-450 B.C.) is beset by uncertainty and, as a result, the subject of much conjecture.[1] It is agreed, however, that private ownership of landed property existed before the time of the *Twelve Tables*.[2] Some scholars hold that ownership of property was originally communal or tribal, later familial, and eventually individual.[3]

When property ownership was in its tribal stage, individuals owned property in the name of the tribe. The amount of property and the length of tenure was determined according to the needs of the group and its rate of productivity. Further grants of land were given by the tribal chieftain on the same basis. According to this tenure, the local chieftain could neither alienate the property nor will it to his children or heirs. His right to the property was personal, vicarious, and inalienable.[4]

In accord with the generally accepted theory, tenure according to the tribe was followed by tenure according to the family. Again the property was given to the chieftain, but usually it was held

---

[1] Jolowicz, p. 1.

[2] Jolowicz, p. 140; Fernand Bernard, *First Year of Roman Law*, translated by Charles P. Sherman (Cambridge, 1906), pp. 186, 187.

[3] Jolowicz, *loc. cit.* Cf. also Edouard Cuq, *Les Institutions Juridiques des Romains* (2 vols., Paris, 1891), I, 75-76 (hereafter cited as Cuq); James Muirhead, *Historical Introduction to the Private Law of Rome* (3. ed., revised by Alexander Grant, London, 1916), pp. 33-37.

[4] Cuq, I, 75.

for life and passed to the chief's male heirs. The property reverted to the tribe only if the head of the family died without issue. In brief, the property was given to the head of the family as a representative of the *family,* and the element of inheritability distinguished familial property from tribal property.[5]

Tenure by means of familial property ultimately developed into tenure by means of individual property, wherein all the previously attached restrictions disappeared and the proprietor could dispose of his property as he chose; he could alienate it or will it to anyone he chose.[6] Edouard Cuq summarized this doctrine of tribal, familial, and individual ownership of property thus:

> We believe . . . that the Romans have passed through, as the other peoples of antiquity, the two phases of an agrarian community and familial property, and that individual ownership of land is separated very slowly from the restrictions introduced by custom in the interest of the family, and traces of which we find among the jurisconsults of the third century of our era.[7]

---

[5] Cuq, *loc. cit.* Cf. also Jolowicz, p. 140.

[6] This tripartite tenure of property paralleled the legendary foundation of the city of Rome. Romulus divided the property into (1) the *ager publicus,* which was state property to be used by the state and its institutions [cf. Adolph Berger, *Encyclopedic Dictionary of Roman Law* (Philadelphia: The American Philosophical Society, 1953), p. 357, s.v. *ager publicus* (hereafter cited as *EDRL*)]. This was largely conquered land, but it could be assigned, leased, or sold to private individuals. He also formed the (2) *heredium* [cf. *EDRL,* p. 486, s.v. *heredium*] which was a plot of ground, the size of two Roman acres (iugera) which had been allotted to the citizens as homesteads. The *heredium* was inalienable, indivisible, and assured to heirs. The third division of property was (3) the *ager gentilicius* [cf. Cuq, I, 90, 91], which was not exclusively composed of fields pertaining to the *gentes* before the foundation of the city, but also included such conquered territory as was given to a *gens.*

[7] Cuq, I, 78. "Nous croyons . . . que les Romains ont traversé, comme les autres peuples de l'antiquité, les deux phases de la communauté agraire et de la propriété familiale, et que la propriété individuelle du sol s'est dégagée très lentement des restrictions introduites par l'usage dans l'interêt de la famille, et dont on trouve la trace jusque chez les jurisconsultes du troisième siècle de notre ère." Cf. also C. W. Westrup, *Introduction to Early Roman Law, Comparative Sociological Studies* (5 vols. in 3, London, 1934-1950), II, 157, for a confirmation of this opinion.

## SECTION II. THE RIGHT OF OWNERSHIP AT THE TIME OF THE TWELVE TABLES

The ownership of landed property may be characterized as a gradually developing institute. Before the *Twelve Tables* ownership of property became subject to law as people became less nomadic and more agricultural.[8] At the time of the *Twelve Tables* individual ownership existed. One held property in his own name and not in the name of the tribe or family. Yet it must be said that the origin of ownership or the title to a particular piece of property was not considered as determinative of ownership at that time. Jolowicz[9] noted that in an action to assert a right of ownership (*rei vindicatio*) the defendant did not need to show how he came into possession, that is, there was no need for him to show title. So long as the plaintiff could not prove his claim (show his title), possession rested with the defendant. The distinction between ownership and possession had not yet been made.[10] Although ownership of landed property was regarded as absolute,[11] nevertheless, restrictions on the rights of property did exist and were incorporated into the *Twelve Tables*. These restrictions were of a twofold nature, public and private. Public restrictions were imposed upon landowners for reasons of public interest or utility.[12] These regulations controlled the extreme limits of property,[13] the overhanging branches of a neighbor's tree,[14] the

[8] Cf. *supra*, footnote 7.

[9] P. 144.

[10] Cf. Jolowicz, p. 272.

[11] Fritz Schulz, *Principles of Roman Law*, translated by Marguerite Wolff (Oxford: The University Press, 1936), p. 152; Jolowicz, p. 142.

[12] ". . . Nulla iuris ratio aut aequitatis benignitas patitur ut quae salubriter pro utilitate hominum introducuntur ea nos duriore interpretatione contra ipsorum commodum producamus ad severitatem."—D.(1.3)25.

[13] Tab. VIII.27: "*Gaius (1.4 ad 1.XII tab.) D.(47.22)4:* His (sodalibus) potestatem facit lex (sc. XII tab.) pactionem quam velint sibi ferre, dum ne quid ex publica lege corrumpant; sed haec lex videtur ex lege Solonis translata esse."—*Fontes Iuris Romani Anteiustiniani* (edd. S. Riccobono, J. Baviera, C. Ferrini, J. Furlani, V. Arrangio-Ruiz, 3 vols. editio altera, Florentiae: A. G. Barbèra, 1941-1943), I, 63 (hereafter cited as *FIRA*).

Tab. VII.2: "*Gaius (L.IV ad L.XII tab.) D.(10.1)13: (10.1).* Sciendum est in actione finium regundorum illud observandum esse, quod (in XII Tab.) ad exemplum quoddammodo eius legis scriptum est quam Athenis Solonem dicitur tulisse."—*FIRA*, I, 48.

[14] Tab. VII.9: "*a. Ulpianus, D.(43.27)1.8:*—lex XII Tab. efficere voluit,

fruit which had fallen from a neighbor's tree on one's own land,[15] and, lastly, the preservation of the natural flow of water.[16] Other restrictions belonged to the sphere of private law because they concerned the vested rights of other parties as opposed to those which the state imposed because of their public nature.

At the time of the *Twelve Tables* these private restrictions were five in number: *via, iter, actus, rivus,* and *cloaca.*[17]

The restrictions which were established by private law at the time of the *Twelve Tables* give an indication of their later development into the various kinds of servitudes which were protected by interdicts.[18] The interdicts came into being only with the establishment of the praetorship in 367 B.C.,[19] so that in the century intervening between the promulgation of the *Twelve Tables* (451-450 B.C.) and the creation of the praetorship these forerunners of the servitudes of the later periods formed whatever restraint existed of the exercise of the right of private ownership.

The first of these restraints is the *iter* or *ius itineris.*[20] *Iter* is

---

ut XV pedes altius rami arboris circumcidantur.—*b. Pomponius, D(43.27)2:* Si arbor ex vicini fundo vento inclinata in tuum fundum sit, ex lege XII Tab. de adimenda ea recta agere potes."—*FIRA,* I, 50.

[15] Tab. VII.10.: "*Plinius n.h. 16, 5,15:* Cautum est—lege XII Tabularum, ut glandem in alienum fundum procidentem liceret colligere."—*FIRA,* I, 50, 51.

[16] Tab. VII.8.: "a. Si aqua pluvia nocet. . . .—*b. Paulus D.(43.8)5:* Si per publicum locum rivus aquae ductus privato nocebit, erit actio privato ex lege XII Tabularum, ut noxa domino caveatur."—*FIRA,* I, 50. Cf. also D.(40.7)21.

[17] Jolowicz, p. 159, Cuq, I, 271.

[18] Cf. *infra,* pp. 13, 14.

[19] Jolowicz, p. 15.

[20] D(8.3)1. pr.: "*Ulpianus libro secundo institutionum.* Servitutes praediorum rusticorum sunt hae: iter, actus, via, aquae ductus. Iter est ius eundi, ambulandi homini, non etiam iumentum agendi. Actus est ius agendi vel iumentum vel vehiculum: itaque qui iter habet, actum non habet, qui actum habet, et iter etiam sine iumento. Via est ius eundi et agendi et ambulandi: nam et iter et actum in se via continent, Aquae ductus est ius aquam ducendi per fundum alienum." Cf. also D.(43.19)1.; *EDRL,* p. 517, s.v. *iter.*

a rustic praedial servitude[21] entitling the beneficiary thereof to pass through (*ius eundi*), to walk through (*ius ambulandi*), and to ride on horseback through another's land.[22] *Actus* was a similar servitude which gave the right to drive a draft animal or vehicles through another's property.[23] A combination of these rights was included in the right of *via,* wherein one had full right to pass through, to drive draft animals or vehicles through another's land. That this right was considered more important than either *iter* or *actus* is demonstrated by the fact that special provisions were made by law for its width,[24] which was not true either of *iter* or *actus.* The last rustic servitude was *rivus.*[25] A rivus was a brook, a stream or any lesser body of flowing water.[26] It also included a ditch or channel whereby water ran from one man's property to that of another. From this fact and circumstance developed the right of *ius aquae* or *aquae ductus.*[27] By means of the former, one obtained the right of taking water flowing through another's property, and by the latter, the right of constructing a private aqueduct on another's property.

---

[21] Jolowicz, p. 159 and Cuq, I, 271, cite four praedial servitudes from this period: *iter, rivus, aqua,* and *actus. Cloaca* is the only urban servitude of this period.

[22] Cf. D.(8.3)1. pr.

[23] "*Modestinus libro nono differentiarum.* Inter actum et iter nonnulla est differentia: iter est enim, qua quis pedes vel equus commeare potest, actus vero, ubi et armenta traicere et vehiculum ducere liceat."—D.(8.3)12.

[24] "*Iavolenus libro decimo ex Cassio:* Latitudo actus itinerisque ea est, quae demonstrata est: quod si nihil dictum est, hoc ab arbitro statuendum est. In via aliud iuris est: nam si dicta latitudo non est, legitime debetur. Si locus non adiecta latitudine nominatus est, per eum qualibet iri poterit: sin autem praetermissus est aeque latitudine non adiecta, per totum fundum una poterit eligi via dumtaxat eius latitudinis, quae lege comprehensa est, pro quo ipso, sin dubitabitur, arbitri officium invocandum est."—D.(8.3)13.2.3. Cf. also D.(43.19)3.15 and *EDRL,* p. 763, s.v. *via.*

[25] "*Servius ad Ulpianum, I. LXX ad Edictum:* . . . Servius et Labeo scribunt, si rivum, qui ab initio terrenus fuit, quia aquam non continebat, cementicium velit facere, audiendum esse: sed et si eum rivum, qui structibilis fuit, postea terrenum faciat aut per partem rivi, aeque non esse prohibendum. . . ."—D.(43.21)3.1.

[26] *EDRL,* p. 686, s.v. *rivus.*

[27] *Ius aquae:* cf. D.(43.20; C.(3.34); *EDRL,* p. 365, s.v. *aqua. Aquae ductus:* cf. C.(11.43); *EDRL,* p. 365, s.v. *aquae ductus.*

The only urban servitude of this period was the *ius cloacae immittendae.*[28] A *cloaca* was a sewer or drain.[29] It is known that a canalized stream drained the northeastern part of Rome from the Argiletum to the Tiber by way of the Forum Romanum and Velabrum. Its regulation was traditionally ascribed to Tarquinius Superbus, and branch drains of the fifth century did exist.[30] Jolowicz notes that the *ius cloacae immittendae* may have arisen after the sack of Rome in 390 B.C. by the Senones (Gauls).[31] It is known that many of the sewers existing in Rome during classical times date partly to the third century before Christ.[32] Hence it is possible that the sewers of the third century before Christ were built after the sack of 390 B.C.

A further consideration is a text of Livy (59 B.C.-A.D. 17) which related that the Roman Senate was considering moving the Capital to Veies after the sack of Rome but decided to remain at Rome after receiving an omen. Livy continued:

> . . . [P]eople began in a random fashion to rebuild the City. . . . In their haste men were careless about making straight the streets and, paying no attention to their own and others' rights, built on the vacant spaces. This is the reason that the ancient sewers, which were at first conducted through the public ways, at present frequently run under private buildings, and the appearance of the City is like one where the ground has been appropriated rather than divided.[33]

---

[28] Jolowicz, p. 159; Cuq, I, 271; "*Ulpianus libro decimo tertio ad legem Iuliam et Papiam.* Ius cloacae mittendae servitus est."—D.(8.1)7.

[29] Cf. *EDRL,* p. 391, s.v. *cloaca.*

[30] *Oxford Classical Dictionary* (edited by M. Cory, A. D. Nock, J. D. Dennison, J. Wight Duff, W. D. Ross, H. H. Scullard, London: Oxford University Press, 1949), s.v. *cloaca maxima.*

[31] Jolowicz, p. 159, footnote 2.

[32] *Oxford Classical Dictionary, loc. cit.*

[33] ". . . urbs aedificari coepta. . . . Festinatio curam exemit vicos dirigendi, dum omisso sui alienique discrimine in vacuo aedificant. Ea est causa ut veteres cloacae, prius per publicum ductae, nunc privata passim subeant tecta, formaque urbis sit occupatae magis quam divisae similis."—Livy, V, 55, 1-5. *Historiae,* in 13 vols., translated by B. O. Foster, Loeb Classical Library (New York, 1924), vol. III, pp. 186, 187.

It seems, then, that in the rebuilding of the City of Rome the drain of one man's house frequently had to pass under and through the property of another man in order to be connected to the main sewerage system. It also seems that the right to construct and maintain such a drain, a restraint of another man's ownership, resulted from the haphazard rebuilding of the city.

### SECTION III. THE RIGHT OF OWNERSHIP IN CLASSICAL LAW

With the institution of the Praetorship in 367 B.C. a further development affected the restraint of the right of ownership. Jolowicz noted that the elaboration of the absolute concept of ownership and the differentiation of possession as distinct from ownership became evident through the growth of the praetorian interdicts, especially the possessory interdicts.[34] These possessory interdicts protected possession as an existing state of fact, irrespective of how possession was attained. Even the rightful owner, if he did not have possession, had to institute judicial proceedings against the possessor in order to vindicate his title.[35]

The growing restraints upon private ownership in substantive Roman Private Law fell into two groups: limitations imposed by the rights of neighbors, and limitations engendered by the previous voluntary action on the part of the owner or his predecessor—servitudes.[36]

The rights of neighbors in part determined the limitations and restrictions imposed upon ownership. Besides any actions founded on servitudes there were four general proceedings which aimed at securing land and buildings against danger or injury. These proceedings were based on the natural claim of an owner or other interested person that "his neighbors or others shall not interfere injuriously with his land, or work their own land, or so omit to repair their buildings, as to put the former to unnecessary loss or peril."[37]

---

[34] Jolowicz, p. 272.

[35] Jolowicz, *loc. cit.;* Fritz Schulz, *Classical Roman Law,* p. 445.

[36] Henry John Roby, *Roman Private Law in the Times of Cicero and the Antonines* (2 vols., Cambridge, 1902), I, 414 (hereafter cited as Roby).

[37] Roby, I, 509.

These four proceedings were *cautio damni infecti, aquae arcendae pluviae actio, operis novi nuntiatio,* and the *interdictum quod vi aut clam.*[38]

*Cautio damni infecti:* If harm had not yet occurred but threatened one's property from some activity of his neighbor or by the defective state of the latter's property, the damage was considered as done and relief was given to the plaintiff. This effectively constrained the defendant to act in a way that was not prejudicial to the interests of the plaintiff.[39]

*Aquae pluviae arcendae actio:* This was an action to restrain an owner of higher land from diverting the natural flow of rain water by any action on his part. The purpose of the action was to restore the previous condition and to reimburse the plaintiff (owner of lower land) for any damages suffered while the action was in progress.[40]

*Operis novi nuntiatio:* This was a protestation by an owner of land or other immovable object against construction by a neighbor on the latter's property which would interfere with the right of the owner to use his own property. The defendant was compelled either to discontinue construction, or to give security to the plaintiff that he (the plaintiff) would suffer no damages from the construction, or to guarantee that the original conditions would be restored.[41]

*Interdictum quod vi aut clam:* This interdict might be granted when a plaintiff requested the praetor to command the defendant to desist from some project which the latter had undertaken on the plaintiff's property. The purpose of the interdict was the restitution of the original status or condition by the defendant himself or at his expense. This interdict was so named because it concerned anything done by force or stealth within a year's time after the project had been undertaken. That the plaintiff had a right to undertake the project was not material to the granting

---

[38] Roby, *loc. cit.*

[39] Cf. D.(39.2)7; Jolowicz, pp. 235-237; *EDRL,* p. 424, s.v. *damnum infectum.*

[40] Cf. D.(39.3)3.4 and D.(39.4)6.6; cf. also Roby, I, 515-517.

[41] Cf. D.(39.1)1.14.3; cf. also Roby, I, 517-520; *EDRL,* p. 609, s.v. *operis novi nuntiatio.*

of the interdict. It was a peremptory interference on the part of the court preliminary to a sentence definitive of the rights of the parties at suit.[42]

In addition to these special measures which restrained the exercise of rights in civil procedure and the limitations imposed upon owners by the rights of neighbors, there remained those limitations which arose from agreements between the parties or other private acts that brought about an interest in land on the part of a non-owner. These were the servitudes, some of which were special rights protected by the *Twelve Tables*[43] and developed into the substantive law under the category of servitudes.

In Roman Law, property is the absolute, exclusive, and perpetual right to something, in the case of real property, to the land.[44] For practical purposes *proprietas* and *dominium* were identical.[45] They were different aspects of the one reality. One (*proprietas*) dealt with the static element of ownership, and the other (dominium) was concerned with its dynamic element.[46]

A servitude was a limitation of the right of property of another or a right over the property of another. A servitude was never defined in Roman Law,[47] but it was described as a *ius in re aliena.*[48] In the time of Justinian (527-565) a servitude was defined as a "passive burden," and this, of course, imposed upon a corporeal thing by a private legal act concerning the use of that thing.[49] It must be said, however, that the jurists of the classical

---

[42] "Quod vi aut clam factum est, qua de re agitur, id si non plus quam annus est cum experiendi potestas est, restituas."—D.(43.24)1.pr.; cf. also C.(8.2) and *EDRL,* p. 511, s.v. *Interdictum quod vi aut clam.*

[43] Cf. *supra,* footnote 17.

[44] Fritz Schulz, *Principles of Roman Law,* p. 152; Jolowicz, p. 142. See also Sosius d'Angelo, *Ius Digestorum* (2 vols., Romae, 1927), II, 28 (hereafter cited as d'Angelo).

[45] ". . . dominium . . . id est proprietas . . ."—D.(41.1)13; "Domini appellatione continetur qui habet proprietatem, etsi usufructuarius alienus sit."—D.(29.5)1.1. *Proprietas* was a term of later origin than *dominium.*

[46] D'Angelo, II, 15.

[47] D'Angelo, II, 186.

[48] ". . . in ea re ius habeant. . . ."—D.(9.4)30; cf. also D.(39.2)19 and D.(47.8)2.22 for identical phraseology.

[49] D.(8.1)15.1. Cf. Schulz, *Classical Roman Law,* p. 381.

age of Roman Law had already understood the bases of this concept, which were expressed in three principles:

1. *"Nemini res sua servit."*—Roman Law considered *dominium* to be the supreme and unlimited right over a thing. *Dominium* contained all limited rights. This principle was used to denote what rights of an estate were not servient to the servitude.[50]

2. *"Servitus in faciendo consistere nequit."*—Since a servitude by its nature was a *ius in rem,* i.e., a limitation of the property rights of another person, an obligation on the part of the owner or a *ius in personam* could not arise from a servitude.[51]

3. *"Servitus servitutis esse non potest."*—This principle embodies the Roman doctrine that a right cannot have another right for its object.[52]

From these general principles and the several texts included in the *Digest* of Justinian one may conclude that a servitude was a true *limitation* of the property rights of another, which property was always supposed; that a servitude was extinguished if the two rights (the right of property and the right of servitude) were vested in the same person;[53] that a servitude could be established only in behalf of the economic usefulness of some active subject;[54] and that in the establishment of a servitude the certain and definite specification of the recognized juridic connection between the right of property (servient estate) and the right of servitude (dominant estate) be made; otherwise a general declaration effected nothing.[55]

---

[50] "*Paul. I. XV ad Sab.:* In re communi nemo dominorum iure servitutis neque facere quicquam invito altero potest neque prohibere, quo minus alter faciat: nulli enim res sua servit. . . ."—D.(8.2)26.

[51] "*Pompon. I. XXXIII ad Sab.:* Servitutium non ea natura est, ut aliquid faciat quis, veluti viridia tollat aut amoeniorum prospectum praestet, aut in hoc ut in suo pingat, sed ut aliquid patiatur aut non faciat."—D.(8.1)15.1. A single notable exception was the *servitus oneris ferendi* (cf. *infra,* p. 21, footnote 72).

[52] "*Paul. I. III ad Sab.:* Nec usus nec usus fructus itineris actus viae acqueductus legari potest, quia servitus servitutis esse non potest."—D.(33.2)1. Cf. also D.(8.3)23.1.

[53] This was *confusio* or *consolidatio;* cf. D.(8.2)30 and also *EDRL,* pp. 407 and 409.

[54] D.(8.1)15, *supra,* footnote 51.

[55] ". . . species servitutis exprimenda est. . . ."—D.(8.4)7.

Servitudes were of two kinds in Roman Law, real (praedial) and personal. Praedial servitudes were divided into rustic and urban servitudes.[56]

A praedial servitude was a right of use over an estate in land of another. In Roman Law an abstract conception of a praedial servitude did not exist, perhaps, until post-classical times.[57] In classical law praedial servitudes were considered primarily in their concrete circumstances. As a general rule they followed these principles:

1. Since a servitude presupposed the property of another because *nemini res sua servit,* it followed that, if the dominant estate ceased to have an owner, the servitude was extinguished; not, however, if the servient estate lacked an owner.[58]

2. The subjects of servitudes were the estates themselves. Thus it was required that the servitudes afford some utility to the dominant estate, and not merely to the person of the estate-holder. It was required, moreover, that servitudes be restricted to the needs of the dominant estate.[59] It followed, then, that the estate could indeed be alienated together with the servitude, but the servitude alone could not be alienated separately from the estate.[60]

3. Since a servitude was considered as an extension or a limitation of ownership, it must have been considered, as ownership itself was considered, essentially perpetual. This perpetuity was evident because, on the one hand, a servitude was not usually established ad tempus,[61] and, on the other hand, a *causa perpetua* was required in all real or praedial servitudes.[62]

---

[56] "*Marcian. 1. III regul.:* Servitutes aut personarum sunt, ut usus et ususfructus, aut rerum, ut servitutes rusticorum praediorum et urbanorum." —D.(8.1); but this text is interpolated. Cf. Fritz Schulz, *Classical Roman Law,* p. 385 and d'Angelo, II, 192.

[57] Cf. d'Angelo, II, 194.

[58] D'Angelo, *loc. cit.*

[59] On these two points cf. D.(8.1)8.: ". . . ut pomum decerpere liceat et ut spaticri et ut cenare in alieno possimus, servitus imponi non potest . . ." and D.(8.3)5.1: "Non ultra posse quam quatenus ad eum ipsum fundum opus sit."

[60] Cf. D.(8.3)36.

[61] Cf. D.(8.1)4.

[62] Cf. D.(8.2)28. This was true at least in all servitudes of water, as is seen in D.(8.3)9.1.

Of the praedial servitudes, the rustic servitudes were as a rule *res mancipi,* and urban servitudes were, conversely, *res nec mancipi.*[63] It has been seen that the oldest rustic servitudes were *iter, actus,* and *via,* to which were added *aqua* and *aquaeductus.*[64] Among those rustic servitudes which were recognized in the classical period were *ius aquae haustus,*[65] *ius pecoris ad aquam adpulsus* and *ius pascendi,*[66] *arenae fodiendae, cretae eximendae,*[67] and *calcis coquendae.*[68]

Urban servitudes, with the exception of *ius cloacae immittendae,* came into being after the institution of the praetorship. In the classical period three classes of urban servitudes were recognized.[69]

1. *Iura stillicidiorum* included the *servitus cloacae immittendae,*[70] the *servitus stillicidii* (with its contradictory), and the *servitus fluminum* (with its contradictory).[71]

2. *Iura parietum* included the servitudes *tigni immittendi, oneris ferendi, proiiciendi vel protegendi.*[72]

---

[63] Fritz Schulz, *Classical Roman Law,* p. 395; cf. also D.(8.3)2.pr.

[64] Cf. *supra,* pp. 8-10.

[65] Cf. D.(8.3)3.3. and *EDRL,* p. 703, s.v. *Servitus aquae haustus.* This servitude gave the right to take water from a fountain, pond, spring, or well located on a neighbor's property. *Iter* was also included.

[66] Cf. D.(8.3)4 and *EDRL,* p. 531, s.v. *ius pascendi.* These two rights were often held simultaneously (D'Angelo, II, 197). They included the right to bring sheep and cattle to water and the right to graze.

[67] Cf. D.(8.3)6.1 and *EDRL,* p. 703, s.v. *Servitus arenae fodiendae.* This servitude was the right to dig for sand in land belonging to another. *Cretae eximendae* entitled one to take chalk from another's soil.

[68] Cf. D.(8.3)5.1 and *EDRL, loc. cit.,* s.v. *servitus calcis coquendae.* This servitude allowed the burning of lime on another's land.

[69] "Fluvius, quod fluit, item flumen: a quo lege praediorum urbanorum scribitur: Stillicidia fluminaque uti nunc, ut ita cadant fluantque. . . ."—Varro, V. 27. *De Lingua Latina,* translated in 2 vols. by Roland G. Kent, Loeb Classical Library (New York, 1924), I, 26, 27.

[70] Cf. D.(8.1)7 and (43.23)8.

[71] Cf. D.(8.2)2 and *EDRL,* pp. 703, 704, s.v. *servitus stillicidii. Stillicidia* included the right to discharge, divert or collect rainwater.

[72] Cf. D.(8.5)6.2 and 8; also D.(50.16)242.1, and *EDRL, loc. cit.* The *ius tigni immittendi* granted one the right to introduce a beam into the wall of a neighbor's building to strengthen one's own building. The *ius oneris ferendi* gave the right to have one's building supported by the neighbor's wall, which wall was to be kept in good repair. Also included were rights of balcony and roof over another's land.

3. *Iura parietum* included *servitutes luminum* also. These were the *servitutes altius tollendi, luminibus officiatur, prospectui officiatur* to which were added *sterculinii* and *fumi immittendi.*[73]

The last group of servitudes were the personal servitudes. These restrictions of the exercise of one's right belonged to the person who held the servitude. Personal servitudes differed from praedial servitudes in structure, inasmuch as the relationship was not between two estates but between a person and a thing. Lastly, they differed in function, because the personal servitude directly afforded service not to the estate but to the person. Furthermore, in a praedial servitude the object was only a *res immobilis,* whereas the object of a personal servitude might also be a *res mobilis.* Again, while every praedial servitude was individual and indivisible, a personal servitude was divisible.[74]

Among the principal personal servitudes were usufruct, quasi-usufruct, *usus, habitatio,* and *servitus operarum.*[75] Usufruct, as a rule, applied only to non-fungible goods which were not consumed in use.[76] Quasi-usufruct gave the right to consume fungible goods,[77] to which right was coupled the obligation of restoring goods of similar quality and quantity or their value. Usus had limited application, for example, where a family had the use of a farmhouse, but not of the land on which the farmhouse stood.[78] *Habitatio* and *servitus operarum* were regarded as forms of *usus* in classical law, but were considered separately in the time of Justinian.[79] The titleholder of the *servitus habitationis* could not grant habitation gratuitously to another, but he could rent the dwelling.[80] *Habitatio* also differed from *usus* in post-

[73] Cf. D.(8.2)4; (8.2)12; (8.5)17.2 and (8.5)8.5. These restrictions concerned rights over sunlight and views. One had the right to estop another from building in such a way on his own property. These servitudes made allowance also for contradictory rights.

[74] Cf. *Institutiones,* 2.4-5; D.(7.1)8; D.(7.1)49 and 50; C.(3.33).

[75] "Usufructus est ius alienis rebus utendi, fruendi, salva rerum substantia." —*Institutiones,* 2.4.

[76] ". . . res quae numero, pondere, mensura consistunt. . . ."—D.(12.1)2.1.

[77] Cf. *Inst.* II, 4, 2.

[78] ". . . cui usus relictus est uti potest, frui non potest. . . ."—D.(7.8)1.2.

[79] F. Schulz, *Classical Roman Law,* 391.

[80] Cf. *Institutiones,* 2.5.5.

classical law, inasmuch as *habitatio* was recovered as often as it was exercised as a right. Finally, the *servitus operarum* was the right of receiving the aid of another's slave or animals.[81]

## SECTION IV. THE RIGHT OF OWNERSHIP IN POST-CLASSICAL LAW

The law of servitudes was fully developed by the end of the classical era of Roman Law. Additional restrictions were, nevertheless, added to the right of property in the post-classical period.[82] The emphasis shifted from a delineation of the objective right to an analysis of the subjective morality which underlay the objective right. With the influence of Christianity this new emphasis grew and came to harass Roman lawyers in the late Middle Ages. Nowhere was this shift more evident than in the "abuse" of the exercise of one's rights, or the theory of emulative acts.[83]

The term *aemulatio* was known to Cicero (106 B.C.-43 B.C.) in a twofold sense, but its juridic meaning derived from the jurist, Macerius.[84] The following case may be supposed as illustrative of this institute: A has a right. He exercises his right in such a way that no advantage or utility accrues to himself. A's intention in exercising his right is the working of harm upon his neighbor, B. This harm is actually wrought, yet without infringing upon any right of B, A's neighbor.

One may arrive at a descriptive definition of an emulative act as any act which an agent performs according to law, that is, as an exercise of his own subjective right, but which act is legally restrained because the intention of the agent is to cause distress

---

[81] ". . . si operae hominis vel alicuius animalis relictae fuerint. . . ."—D.(7.9)5.3.

[82] Cf. Jolowicz, p. 519.

[83] Cf. d'Angelo, I, 639-643.

[84] Marcus Tullius Cicero, *Tusculanarum Disputationum Libri Quinque,* ed. by Thomas W. Dougan and Robert M. Henry (Cambridge, 1934), p. 122. Cicero, *Disputationes Tusculanae,* IV, 8, 17: "Aemulatio autem dupliciter quidem dicitur . . . [est] imitatio virtutis . . . et aemulatio aegritudo, si eo, quod concupierit, alius potiatur, ipse careat." "*Macerius, Lib. II de officiis praesidis:* Opus novum privato etiam sine principis auctoritate facere licet, praeterquam si ad aemulationem alterius civitatis pertineat. . . ."—D.(50.10)3; see also C.(12.58)1.

or discomfort to one's neighbor, whose rights are in no way infringed upon by the act of the agent.

Classical law stressed the freedom of action which the individual citizen enjoyed in the possession and exercise of his rights. The restraints which existed were in the nature of exceptions to the general law. During this period any investigation of the intention which directed the citizen's exercise of his right was denied and every abuse of his right or its exercise was permitted.[85]

Two exceptions to this general principle are evident in the sources, but by their rarity these exceptions only seem to confirm the existence of the principle.[86] It is the commonly held doctrine, then, that no theory of emulative acts existed in classical law.[87]

That such a theory of emulative acts existed in the time of Justinian is based on two phrases, which appear in the Digest.[88] In a discussion of this theory Buckland and McNair ask the question:

> Was there a rule of Roman law that a man might not exercise his rights merely for the detriment of another, with no economic or betterment aim for himself? The

---

[85] This point of view was derived from the following principles: "Nullus videtur dolo facere, qui suo iure utitur."—D.(50.17)55; "Nemo damnum facit, nisi qui id fecit, quod facere ius non habet."—*Ibid.*, 151; "Dolo malo non videtur habere qui suo iure utitur."—D.(43.29)3.2. For similar expressions, cf. D.(47.10)13.1; (8.2)9; (39.2)26; (50.17)155; (39.12)24.2; (39.2)26; (39.3)21.

[86] ". . . expedit enim rei publicae, ne quis re sua male utatur."—*Institutiones*, 1.8.2; ". . . male enim nostro iure uti non debemus. . . ."—*Gai Institutiones* or *Institutes of Roman Law by Gaius*, with a translation by Edward Poste (4. ed. in 4 Books; revised by E. A. Wittuck, Oxford, 1904), I, 53. Cf. also D.(8.1)9, where it is stated that praedial servitudes were to be exercised *civiliter modo*.

[87] Cf. d'Angelo, I, 640; *EDRL*, p. 353, s.v. *aemulatio*. Cf. also W. W. Buckland and A. D. McNair, *Roman Law and Common Law* (2. ed., revised by F. H. Lawson, Cambridge: The University Press, 1952), p. 97.

[88] ". . . neque malitiis indulgendum est. . . ."—D.(6.1)38; ". . . quae sententia verior est si modo non hoc animo fecit ut tibi noceat, sed ne sibi noceat."—D.(39.3)2.9. Similar expressions are found in D.(39.3)1.12 and (39.3)2.5.

> correct answer seems to be that there was not. The rules for one or two cases expressing this notion are really evidence against, not for, the existence of a general rule. Had there been one the specific rules would not have been needed, and the notion is always stated as an ethical makeweight—a man ought not to do this sort of thing. Nowhere is it said that a principle of law forbids it. On the contrary, we get more than once the proposition that one who is exercising his right cannot be committing a wrong.[89]

In summary, the right of private property always existed as a restricted right in Roman Law. These restrictions were refined and categorized in the classical Roman Law of servitudes. Furthermore, these restrictions were extended beyond the right of property ownership to such rights as the right of marriage, of testation, of the administration of one's goods, of contract, etc. Finally, the civil lawyers of the late Middle Ages brought this concept of the restraint of one's rights into the moral order with the theory of emulative acts. The theory was an attempt by the lawgiver to protect public morality by a legal sanction upon the immoral intention of an agent in the exercise of his lawful rights.

---

[89] Cf. W. W. Buckland and A. D. McNair, *Roman Law and Common Law*, p. 98.

## CHAPTER II

### The Right of Ownership in Germanic Law

Roman Law achieved its classical expression after the birth of Christianity. With the "Edict of Constantine" in 313 Christianity was officially allowed to exist. During the reign of Emperor Theodosius I (346?-395), who came to power in 379, Christianity supplanted paganism as the state religion. The Roman Empire was divided into parts at the death of Theodosius in 395, and in 476 the Western Empire came to an end with the barbarian invasions.[1]

The invasion of the Western Empire by the Visigoths (376), Ostrogoths (493), and Franks (430-460) changed the political structure of Western Europe. Together with an expanding Christian Church these Germanic tribes began to establish political and social institutions, some of which have lasted to our own day.

It will be the purpose of this chapter to outline the Germanic notion of property ownership as a right which suffered legal restrictions. Church property also suffered these restrictions, as will be indicated in the course of this treatment.

#### SECTION I. GENERAL CHARACTER OF GERMANIC LAW

The German tribes generally accepted the political situation in which they found themselves after the barbarian invasions and allowed the power of their Germanic institutions to retain its effect. That the Germanic institutions were powerful, albeit crude, at this time may be seen from the "feudal system" which developed and endured throughout Christendom from the fall of Rome in 476 until the Protestant Reformation in the first half of the Twelfth Century, and even later in Spain and Italy. The Germans ruled themselves with a harsh and crude customary law.[2] These tribes had no concept of the state as any source of legislation, and considered laws (*leges*) not so much as dispositive acts

---

[1] Jolowicz, pp. xx, 43 f.

[2] Ferdinand Lot, *End of the Ancient World and the Beginnings of the Middle Ages* (London, 1931), p. 397.

of government but as recorded customs of the tribe.[3] The law was considered to be the discovery of a truth rather than the imposition of a command. In a case which involved a determination of fact, the ruling lord was unwilling that a question concerning a difference of laws be resolved by an appeal to numbers; rather the lord preferred a battle of champions in which the difference of laws would be resolved in favor of the winner of a joust.[4]

During the sixth and seventh centuries the Frankish kingdom veered between an explosive stability and outright anarchy.[5] When a sovereign died, an inevitable battle concerning succession to his lands began among his heirs. Just as inevitably the battle was ended by a division of the kingdom. The solution to this *impasse* was the formation of *clientèles armées,* a soldiery which offered protection to a lord in return for payments and privileges—usually land. Men ceased to remain free; they became vassals in the service of the lord, who thus became powerful among his peers.

Those less than free men were generally termed *ingenui in obsequio.*[6] Another group of vassals were the *antrustiones,* who formed the palace guard. They promised fidelity to the lord and were granted special protection by law.[7]

---

[3] Edward Jenks, *Law and Politics in the Middle Ages* (New York, 1898), pp. 7, 8.

[4] Jenks, *op. cit.,* p. 9; cf. also *Francisci Pithoei Glossarium Legis Salicae,* tit. XXXV, 6, where the compiler recalls a text of Tacitus: "Tacitus de Moribus Germanorum; 'Aleam sobrii inter seria exercent, et novisimo iactu de libertate et de corpore contendunt. . . .' "—Mansi, *Sacrorum Conciliorum Nova et Amplissima Collectio,* 53 vols. in 60 (Vols. I-XXXV, Florentiae, Vevetiis, 1758-1798; Vols. XXXVI-LX, Parisiis, 1901-1927), Supplementum XVIII, 692 (hereafter cited as Mansi).

[5] François L. Ganshof, *Qu'est-ce que la féodalité?* (2. ed., Neuchatel: Editions de la Baconniere, 1947), p. 16. English translation of 3. ed.: F. L. Ganshof, Feudalism (3. ed., New York: Harper and Brothers, 1961), p. 16.

[6] "Quod si homo aut ingenui in obsequium alterius inculpatus fuerit, ipse qui eum post se eodem tempore retinuit, in praesentia iudicis similiter, sicut superius comprehensum est, repraesentare studiat, aut in rem respondere." —Lex Ripuaria, tit. V, 31.1; *Monumenta Germaniae Historica, Series Legum,* inde ab anno Christi 500 usque ad 1500 (5 vols., Hannoverae, 1875-1889), V, 223 (hereafter cited as *M.G.H., Leges*).

[7] *Marculfi Formularum Libri Duo,* Lib. I, c. 18—Mansi Supplementum XVIII, 386; *ibid.,* c. 24; Mansi, Supplementum XVIII, 388.

The juridic act whereby one became a vassal of another was a *commendatio*. Although the *commendatio* was known in the fifth century, it became more common in the sixth and seventh centuries. In effect, a *commendatio* was a contract between the lord and a free man. The lord was limited in his demands upon free men to those demands which were compatible with a free man's station in life.[8] The contract generally stipulated that the lord would offer protection as well as food and clothing to the free man in return for fealty, work, and service.[9] In brief, the *commendatio* was a contract made *intuitu personae*.

Upon the signing of the *commendatio* or upon verbal agreement the lord customarily transferred some property to the vassal for the vassal's maintenance. The lord could cede the property to the vassal totally, but usually ceded only the right of use and enjoyment of the property for a prolonged period of time. This property was called a *beneficium* or benefice[10] when no fixed tax or obligation was attached to the tenure.

One may conclude from this system of property ownership that, in contrast with Roman Law, Germanic Law was a land-institution. It expressed its social relationships by means of land-institutions to such an extent that land-holding became a military system with land as the reward for service, on the one hand, and the base of governmental power, on the other hand.[11]

From its early origins the feudal system understood the benefice and the vassalage as separate and independent entities. In the developing society of the Middle Ages, however, these two institutes were inexorably drawn together and were eventually united in the *feudem* or *fief*.

In order to retain large numbers of armed soldiers Charles Martel (714-741) and Pepin the Short (741-768) had multiplied the number of vassals. These vassals received benefices, of church

---

[8] Cf. Ganshof, *op. cit.*, p. 22. (English translation: pp. 6-9; 26, 27; 30, 31; 43-46.)

[9] The formula of such a contract is found in *M.G.H.*, *Leges*, V, 223.

[10] Ganshof, *op. cit.*, p. 24. (English translation: pp. 9-12; 36-40.)

[11] Jenks, *op. cit.*, p. 23; Ganshof, *op. cit.*, p. 24. (English translation: pp. 11; 22, 23.)

property in many instances, as a means of securing their services. These usurpations put the Frankish Church in a grave situation. To meet this crisis, councils were held at Estinnes (743) and Hainaut (743). The pertinent provisions of these two councils were collected and included in the Council of Lestines (745):

> . . . We decree also . . . because of the imminent wars and persecutions of the nations which surround us, that we shall retain a part of the Church's lands and patrimony under our protection and custody for the benefit of our army and with the blessing of Almighty God. We issue this decree with this condition, namely, that in each and every year a payment of twelve denarii be made by every estate to the church or monastery from which the land was taken. . . . And likewise, if necessity should demand, or the prince should order it, that this same protective custody be renewed.[12]

Supposedly, the lords and bishops agreed that the lands were to be restored to the Church after the crisis had passed. The lands were to be held *sub praecario,* a recognition of the native right of the Church, and with a yearly payment as a token of recognition of the right of the Church by the vassal. Factually, the lands were never restored because the "necessity" never passed. Charlemagne (742-814) became king in 768, and under his hand the separability of benefice and vassal disappeared altogether.[13]

Another change had taken place in the tenure of the benefice by the end of the ninth century. The rights of the two parties (the lord and the beneficiary) to the *beneficium* usually provided an

---

[12] ". . . statuimus quoque . . . propter imminentia bella et persecutiones ceterarum gentium, quae in circuitu nostro sunt, ut sub praecario et censu aliquam partem ecclesialis pecuniae in adiutorium exercitus nostri, cum indulgentia Dei, aliquanto tempore retineamus, ea conditione ut annis singulis de unaquaque casata solidus, i.e., XII denarii, ad ecclesiam vel monasterium reddantur. . . . Et iterum, si necessitas cogat, aut princeps iubeat, precarium renovetur."—C. 3, Concilium Liptinense; Mansi, XII, 371. *M.G.H., Leges,* t. II, p. 7. (Translation is the writer's.)

[13] Ganshof, *op. cit.,* pp. 16-34, gives a historical treatment of the development of feudalism with bibliographical references. (English translation: pp. 11, 12; 17; 20-50.)

estate for the life of the tenant (beneficiary). Upon the death of the tenant the estate reverted to the lord, who might cede the estate again to another vassal. The strong tendency toward hereditary possession among the vassals, however, effectively restrained the contractual right of the lord to confer the *beneficium* freely upon the death of the beneficiary. Even during the life of the beneficiary, the lord could deprive him of his *beneficium* only if the beneficiary defaulted on his obligations.[14] In any other circumstances the beneficiary had at least the right to be compensated for the loss of his benefice or to be enriched by his promotion to a better benefice.[15]

One may conclude that this restriction of the rights of the lord in favor of the vassal was a consequence of the effective detention of the *beneficium* by the vassal and his desire to assign the property to his heirs. These attempts to restrain contracted rights of the lords demonstrated the innate propensity in man to own his own property and to cede it to anyone he chose.

## SECTION II. GERMANIC LAW AND CANON LAW

### *Article 1. Early Councils*

The usurpation of church lands in the Frankish kingdom during the eighth and ninth centuries under the pretext of political necessity placed the Frankish Church in a serious situation. The Church, in meeting the threatening appropriation of its property, was forced to reflect upon its right of ownership and tenure of property. This problem was placed in focus by Gratian and given a philosophical ground for solution by the later scholastic legal philosophers;[16] the principles which were to serve for a solution

---

[14] "Natura feudi haec est, ut si princeps investierit capitaneos suos de aliquo, non potest eos devestire sine culpa."—*Libri Feudorum,* liber primus, tit. VII. 2. Corpus Iuris Civilis, suae integritati una cum glossis restitutae 4 vols., Vol. I, *Institutiones,* Lugduni, 1549, Vol. II. *Digestum Vetus,* Lugduni, 1550, Vol. III, *Codex,* Lugduni, 1549 *Authenticum, III Libri, Libri Feudorum,* Lugduni, 1550.

[15] Ganshof, *op. cit.,* p. 62.

[16] *Infra,* chapter III, pp. 44-53.

to the problem, however, were already implicitly contained in the statements of the Church in the earlier period.

Shortly after Charlemagne came to the throne of the Frankish kingdom, the II Council of Nicaea was held in 787. The Fathers of the Council, in view of the appropriation of church property, decreed in the twelfth disciplinary canon that bishops were not to transfer benefices into the power of civil officials under penalty of invalidity of the contract. Moreover, the Council advised that bishops should alienate church property only to clerics or farmers in the event that alienation became necessary.[17]

The VI Council of Paris (829) reminded bishops that they did not enjoy absolute rights over church property. Recalling previous legislation,[18] the Council held that a bishop should not convert church property to his own use; nor should he encumber church property with useless burdens from which the Church would gain little, and from which the Church might lose much.[19]

Again, the Council of Meaux (845), repeating the Seventh Canon of the Synod of Beauvais (845), warned that any exchange of benefices involving church property should be approached with the greatest circumspection by ecclesiastical authorities. Canon XXIII prescribed, moreover, that past actions should be put aright according to the decree of Pope Hilarius (461-468).[20]

---

[17] ". . . Omnium rerum ecclesiasticorum episcopus curam gerat, et ea administrat tamquam Deo intuente. . . . Ne liceat autem quidquam ex eis sibi vendicate. . . . Sin autem detrimentum affere causetur . . . alienet praedium, sed clericis vel agricolis."—Mansi, XIII, 752; Jean Hardouin, *Acta Conciliorum et Epistolae Decretales ac Constitutiones Summorum Pontificum* (12 vols., Parisiis, 1714-1715), IV, 494 (hereafter cited as Hardouin).

[18] *Canones Apostolorum,* Can. 49; ". . . qui stipem ecclesiae . . . in suos convertit usos, scriba est et pharisaeus, similisque Iudae perdito. . . . Episcopus ecclesiasticarum rerum habeat potestatem, ad dispensandum erga omnes qui indigent. . . ." H. Bruns, *Canones Apostolorum et Conciliorum Saeculorum IV-VII* (2 vols., Berolini, 1839), I, 6; Mansi, XIV, 549; Hardouin, IV, 1307. Cf. also *M.G.H., Leges,* II-II, 622: Capitulum XV quoting St. Jerome, *Commentarium in Matthaeum* VII, col. 218; and Council of Antioch, Caput XXV—Mansi, II, 1328.

[19] Canon XV; Mansi, *loc. cit.;* cf. also cc. XVI-XVIII Mansi, *ibid.,* 550-552; *M.G.H., Leges,* II-II, 622, 623.

[20] "Ut commutationes rerum ecclesiasticorum valde caveantur, et subtilissime, si aliquo modo fieri debent inspiciantur. Quae autem inconsultae

### *Article 2. Pseudo-Isidorian Forgeries*

Sometime after the publication of the Collection of Benedict the Levite (845) and before the appearance of the *Capitula* of Hincmar of Rheims (852), there appeared at Rheims or LeMans a "canonical collection" whose authenticity was accepted in the Church until 1628, when the collection was proved a forgery by the learned Calvinist, David Blondel (1590-1655).[21] The date of authorship is established by the fact that the forgeries quote the Collection of Benedict the Levite and are cited by Hincmar of Rheims in his *Capitula.*

It must be understood that the forgers were reformers at heart and attempted to heighten the authority of their reform with an appeal to antiquity and the practice of the ancient Church. Thus they interpolated authentic texts with appropriate legislation to effect the desired reforms. Among their aims were the reform of ecclesiastical discipline in Gaul and the protection of ecclesiastical property against lay usurpers. According to R. C. Mortimer:

> To this end texts are found or forged stating that all temporal possessions of the Church are sacrosanct, consecrated to God forever, which it is a sacrilege to put to secular uses or to alienate into secular hands.[22]

The documents here cited are largely taken from the *Collectio Hispana* and were genuine. No doubt their presence among forged and interpolated texts is mute evidence of their value.

Specifically, the False-Decretals contained, with reference to church property, canon XXIV of the Council of Antioch (341);[23]

---

sunt factae, iuxta decretum canonicum Papae Hilarii [cf. Synod of Rome, A.D. 465—*M.G.H., Leges,* I-II, 404], quae illicite decessor noster episcopus admiserit, vel ab aliis illicite commissa sunt, ab eo qui successor est, emendentur."—Mansi, XIV, 824; Hardouin, IV, 1487.

[21] A. G. Cicognani, *Canon Law* (2. ed., revised, Westminster, 1934), pp. 243, 244.

[22] *Western Canon Law* (Los Angeles: University of California, 1953), p. 36.

[23] Paulus Hinschius, ed., *Decretales Pseudo-Isidorianae et Capitula Angilramni* (Leipzig, 1863), p. 272; Migne, *Patrologiae Cursus Completus,*

canon XXXI of the so-called IV Council of Carthage (? 419);[24] canons VII and XXII of the Council of Agde (506);[25] canons VII and VIII of the Council of Epaon (517);[26] canons XIV and XVI of the *Capitula* of Blessed Martin of Braga (*ca.* 563);[27] and canon XVI of the IX Council of Toledo (655).[28]

From the various documents cited in the Pseudo-Isidorian forgeries one may conclude that ownership of property in the Church was a very restricted right. In the first place, bishops and abbots were obliged to administer church property, not as owners but as trustees. A trusteeship was in itself a limitation. Secondly, a bishop could not legally alienate church property except in an emergency. Thirdly, even in an emergency a bishop had to discuss the proposed alienation with his fellow bishops of the province before the actual alienation took place. This last restriction applied also to leases and rentals which continued over a long period of time.

### *Article 3. Later Councils*

The tenor of the earlier conciliar legislation and the Pseudo-Isidorian forgeries was continued in the conciliar legislation which preceded the unification of canon law under the aegis of Master

---

*Series Latina* (221 vols., Parisiis, 1844-1855), Vol. CXXX, col. 84 (hereafter cited as *MPL*); H. Bruns, *op. cit.*, I, 86.

[24] "Ut episcopus rebus ecclesiae tamquam commendatis non tamquam propriis utatur."—Hinschius, *op. cit.*, p. 304; *MPL,* CXXX, col. 345.

[25] Hinschius, *op. cit.,* pp. 332, 333; Bruns, *op. cit.,* II, 147, 150; *MPL,* CXXX, col. 400, 402. Canon VII summarizes the legislations: ". . . quod si necessitas compulserit . . . vel usufructus vel indirecta venditione aliquid distrahatur, apud duos vel tres comprovinciales vel vicinos episcopos causa qua necesse sit vendi primitus comprobetur, ut habita discussione sacerdotali, eorum subscriptione quae facta fuerit venditio roboretur, aliter facta venditio vel transactio non valebit."

[26] Hinschius, *op. cit.,* p. 359; H. Bruns, *op. cit.,* II, 168.

[27] ". . . si . . . episcopus vel qui cum eo . . . quolibet actu ecclesiae veniunt in suos sinus colligunt et pauperes fraudant et fame conficiunt, hos enim corripi oportet secundum quod ordinatum fuerit a sancto concilio."—Hinschius, *op. cit.,* p. 429; *MPL,* CXXX, col. 580, 581.

[28] Hinschius, *op. cit.,* p. 399; H. Bruns, *op. cit.,* I, 96; *MPL,* CXXX, col. 525, 526.

Gratian (fl. 1140). From all this legislation there grew an awareness among canonists of a need to discern the nature and ownership of private property, and, more immediately, the nature and ownership of church property. It was from these texts that the problem came forth; it was also from an analysis of these texts that the problem received a solution.

A synod was held at Rome under Pope Leo IV (847-855) in 853. In a *Breviarium* inserted into the acts of the synod the Pope threatened to inflict canonical penalties upon anyone who did not observe the restrictive legislation concerning the alienation of church property.[29]

In the same year the II Provincial Council of Soissons declared that any exchange of church property required the approval of the king. No doubt this was an attempt to control further the activities of the Church.[30]

The III Council of Valence attempted to correct this infringement when, in 855, it commanded that any exchange of church property must be undertaken with the greatest caution. The reason was that such property was offered to God and was the patrimony of the poor. The text of canon XXI is very clear on these points:

> The greatest care must be used in any exchange of church property; on the one hand, either the prescription of the sacred canons should forbid such an exchange, or, on the other hand, fraud or deceit on the part of a few should be so restrained or arrested in matters of this kind that the Church of God be in no wise despoiled of its land and chattels. Since the very goods of the Church are offered to God by the holy faithful, according to the teaching of the ancient fathers, these goods are nothing

---

[29] ". . . ut nullus episcoporum vel sacerdotum rem sui tituli usurpare aut alienare praesumunt: qui quidem hoc fecerit, canonicam sine dubio iubeat ultionem."—Mansi, XIV, 1025; Hardouin, V, 84.

[30] "Postremo quod a quibusdam conservabatur, praefixum est generaliter ab omnibus custodiendum, ne ullae res ecclesiasticae absque regis conniventia commutentur."—Canon XIII; Mansi, XIV, 982; Hardouin, V, 44; *M.G.H., Leges*, I-II, 266.

> else than the donations of the faithful, the patrimony of the poor, and the redemption of sins. If we do not safeguard the ecclesiastical dedication of these goods, we have sinned grievously against those who have offered these goods and against Almighty God, to Whom these goods have been offered.[31]

The IV Ecumenical Council of Constantinople (870) made more explicit the tenor of the past legislation when it forbade that church property be encumbered by a long-term lease which in Roman Law was termed *emphyteusis*.[32]

A council held in Mainz in 888 forbade anyone from retaining, alienating or removing ecclesiastical goods unjustly, that is, contrary to the written law. It further provided that ecclesiastical property which had been unjustly appropriated and held *sub praecario* had forthwith to be returned to the Church as the lawful owner.[33]

---

[31] "Ut de commutationibus rerum ecclesiasticorum diligentissima adhibeatur cura, ut vel iuxta interdictum et obtestationem sacrorum canonum nullatenus fiant, vel certe fraudulentia et nequitia quorundam in hac re ita coerceantur et amputentur, ut ecclesia Dei suis praediis et facultatibus tam impudenter et dolenter minime spolietur. Quia cum ipsae res ecclesiarum a piis et fidelibus Deo oblatae, iuxta antiquorum patrum sententiam nihil sint aliud nisi vota fidelium, patrimonium pauperum, redemptio peccatorum; si eas fideliter et integre ecclesiasticis usibus non defendium, et in eos qui obtulerunt, et in Deum, cui oblatae sunt, gravissimo nos reatu implicamus."—Concilium Valentinum III, canon XXI; Mansi, XV, 11; Hardouin, V, 94. (Translation is the writer's.)

[32] *Concilium Constantinopolitanum IV*, canon XV; Mansi, XVI, 168, 169; Hardouin, V, 905. *Emphyteusis* was a long-term lease of real property for a nominal yearly rental. Cf. C.(4.66)1; Jolowicz, p. 283.

[33] "Ne cui liceat res vel facultates ecclesiis . . . pro quacumque eleemosyna cum iustitia delegatas retentare, alienare, atque subtrahere."—Mansi, XVIII, 66; Hardouin, VI, 405. "De praecariis . . . Si quilibet hominum res ecclesiae per mendacia vel mala ingenia in praecariam sibi acquirere voluerit, et post factas praecarias eadem mendacia ad aures eiusdem ecclesiae rectoris delata fuerint, ipsa ecclesia res suas quae ei mendaciter abstractae fuerint, pleniter absque ullius contradictione omnimodis recipiat. Ille vero qui res suas per eadem mendacia propter cupiditatem ipsius praecariae, eidem ecclesiae tradidit, simili modo in suam recipiat dominationem."—Canon XX; Mansi, XVIII, 69; Hardouin, VI, 408.

### *Article 4. Later Canonical Collections*

No conciliar legislation pertaining to the disposition of church property is available for the tenth and eleventh centuries. The tenor and tradition of previous authentic legislation were maintained by means of private collections, such as those of Regino of Prüm (906), Abbo, Abbot of Fleury (1004), Burchard of Worms (1000-1025), the Collection of Anselm of Lucca (*ca.* 1081), the Collection of Cardinal Deusdedit (*ca.* 1083-1086), and the *Decretum* of Bishop Ivo of Chartres (1091-1116).

Regino of Prüm summarized the Roman Law of alienation as it was contained in the Novels of Justinian. Originally a constitution was enacted in 470 by the Emperors Leo and Anthemius concerning the alienation of church property.[84] Shortly thereafter, in the beginning of the sixth century, a constitution of the Emperor Anastasius,[85] though wider in territorial extension, was less complete than the constitution of 470. It was this constitution of Anastasius which came to be known as the Leonine Constitution. In 535 Justinian issued his constitution which unified all the Roman Law concerning the alienation of church property.[86] This seventh Novel is the source of and gives the true sense of Canon 340 in Regino's collection.[87] It forbade the alienation of immovable church property, such as houses and lands; church property was not to be burdened with special mortgage; and the contracts of sale, donation, exchange and perpetual lease of

---

[84] C.(1.2)14.

[85] C.(1.2)17.

[86] Nov. VII.

[87] "Nulli liceat alienare rem immobilem ecclesiae, sive domum, sive agrum, sive hortum, sive rusticum mancipium, neque creditoribus specialis hypothecae titulo obligate. Alienationis autem verbum continet 'conditionem' (venditionem), donationem, permutationem, et emphyteusis perpetuum contractum . . . omnes sacerdotes ab huiusmodi abstineant, poenas timentes quos Leonina Constitutio minatur."—Cf. C.(1.2)14; Nov. VII, 1; Regino of Prüm, *Reginonis abbatis Prumiensis libri duo de synodalibus causis et disciplinis ecclesiasticis,* ed. by F. G. Wasserschleben (Leipzig, 1840)—but quoted as cited in Migne as *De Ecclesiasticis Disciplinis,* lib. I, canon 340—*MPL,* CXXXII, col. 261; Burchard of Worms, *Decretum,* lib. III, canon 164—*MPL,* CLXI, col. 241; *Capitula* of Ansegisus (827), lib. II, Cap. 29—*MPL,* XCVII, col. 545 (483).

*emphyteusis* were included within the meaning of alienation. The penalties contained in the same Leonine Constitution were invoked upon all ecclesiastics who violated the law. According to the provision made by Roman Law, however, the Church could exchange property with the civil authority by virtue of a pragmatic sanction.[38] The principle that the right to alienate ecclesiastical property rested solely in the bishop was reaffirmed by later compilers,[39] and eventually by the first general council to be held in the West, that of the First Lateran in 1123.[40] No cleric was allowed to alienate his own benefice or any ecclesiastical fief.[41]

---

[38] Nov. VII, 2; Regino of Prüm, lib. I, Canon 341—*MPL,* CXXXII, col. 261.

[39] ". . . nisi (praecaria) ab ecclesiastico rectore petantur. . . ."—Abbo of Fleury (988-996), *Collectio Canonum,* lib. X, Canon VII—*MPL,* CXXXIX, col. 480, 481; Burchard of Worms, *loc. cit.*

"Et quod res ecclesiae non propriae sed communes esse debent. . . ."—*Collectio Anselmi Luccensis,* lib. V, canon 37; F. Thaner, *Anselmi Luccensis collectio canonum una cum collectione minore* (2 vols., Innsbruck, 1906-1915), II, 164; *MPL,* CXLIX, col. 485 ff.

[40] Council of the Lateran, canon 4—Hardouin, VI, 1111; Mansi, XXI, 282.

[41] I Council of the Lateran, canon 22—Hardouin, VI, 1114; Mansi, XXI, 286.

# CHAPTER III

## The Right of Ownership From Gratian to the Council of Trent

### SECTION I. THE RIGHT OF OWNERSHIP

The *Decretum* of Gratian (fl. 1140) attempted to harmonize the discordant canons of previously enacted church law. In regard to property ownership the dilemma to be faced was between vigorous statements on the part of the early Fathers denouncing the abuses of private property, so as almost to condemn it, and contemporary ecclesiastically sanctioned institutions of private property.

The primitive communism of the early Christians, as evidenced in the New Testament,[1] found expression in a letter supposedly written by St. Clement of Rome (91-100) to the Christians of Jerusalem:

> . . . The use of all things that are in the world ought to be common to all men. . . . There was no one among us in need. But all who owned houses or fields sold them and brought the proceeds with anything else they had and laid them at the feet of the Apostles. . . .[2]

Ioannes Teutonicus (+ ca. 1245), commenting on this text in Gratian, reflected the historical perspective in which it was understood in the later Middle Ages when he said: "It seems nevertheless that this was a command because the primitive Church could command this, like continence; but, if this were commanded

---

[1] Acts, 4:32-35.

[2] ". . . Communis est autem usus omnium, quae sunt in hoc mundo, omnibus esse hominibus debuit . . . omnia illis et nobis erant communia, nec quisquam egens erat inter nos. Omnes autem qui domos vel agros possidebant, vendebant eos, et pretia eorum et reliquas res, quas habebant, afferebant, ponentes ante pedes apostolorum. . . ."—C. 12, q. 1, c. 2. (Translation is the writer's.) This letter was spurious. Cf. Paulus Hinschius, *Decretales Pseudo-Isidorianae* (Leipzig, 1863), pp. 65, 66; Mansi, I, 143.

nowadays, it would cripple the state of the universal Church, which ought not to be."[3]

The larger problem was that private property seemed contrary to the natural law in the thinking of mediaeval canonists. The decretists had explained the statement, "According to the natural law all things are common," by a critical analysis of the word "natural." Huguccio (+ 1210) attempted to investigate the word "common"; and this view was included in the gloss of Ioannes Teutonicus.

> . . . Nature . . . means the instinct of nature proceeding from reason, and the law proceeding from this "nature" is called rational equity, and according to this law of nature all things are called common, that is, they are to be shared in time of necessity as in Dist. 47, c. 8.[4]

Ioannes Teutonicus buttressed his argument that property rights were limited in this way by an appeal to authority. In another gloss a few lines further on Ioannes repeated this argument that "common" meant "to be shared in time of need" and claimed the support of Roman Law. "According to the Rhodian law, foodstuffs especially were common in time of peril," and Ioannes gave a reference to the Digest of Justinian.[5] The text of Justinian dealt with a situation in which several merchants were moving goods by ship, and part of the cargo had to be thrown overboard

[3] ". . . videtur tamen quod hoc fuit praeceptum, quia primitiva ecclesia hoc potuit praecipere: sicut continentiam. Sed si hoc hodie praeciperetur, deformaret statum ecclesiae universalis: quod debet non esse . . . vel dic quod praeceptum erat eis qui tunc renuntiaverant propriis, non aliis."—*Glossa Ordinaria* s.v. *praecepimus* ad c. 2, C. XII, q. 1.

[4] "Ius Naturale . . . dicitur instinctus naturae ex ratione proveniens, et ius ex tali natura proveniens dicitur naturalis aequitas, et secundum hoc ius naturae dicuntur omnia communia, idest, communicanda tempore necessitatis, ut Dist. 47, Sicut (Distinctio 47, c. 8)."—*Glossa Ordinaria,* s.v. *Ius naturale,* ad Dist. 1, c. 7.

[5] "Communis omnium: id est, nihil erat proprium alicui in re divino. Vel dic communis, id est, communicanda tempore necessitatis, ut 47 dist. Sicut, 'nam etiam secundum legem Rhodianam, tempore periculi cibaria maxime erant communia ut ff. Ad leg. Rhod. 1.2 cum in eadem nave in fine' [D.(14.2)2.2]."

to avoid shipwreck. In that event each of the merchants would be assessed in proportion to the value of his goods, but not his personal provisions. If such were lacking, each would contribute what he possessed to the common store. Ioannes took this last provision of the Roman law and erected it into a principle of equity.

The relationship between the right to own property and the right use of property was set forth in a letter attributed to St. Ambrose (340-397). It rebuked a rich man for saying that he could do what he liked with his own wealth, it cast serious doubts on his rights to own property at all, and it strongly emphasized his duty to help the poor:

> But you say, "Where is the injustice if I diligently look after my own property without interfering with other people's?" O impudent words! Your own property, you say. What? When you came into the light, when you came forth from your mother's womb, with what resources, with what reserves did you come endowed? No one may call his own what is common, of which, if man takes more than he needs, it is obtained by violence. . . . Who is more unjust, more avaricious, more greedy than a man who takes the food of the multitude not for his own use but for his abundance and luxuries? . . . The bread that you hold back belongs to the needy, the clothes that you shut away belong to the naked, the money that you bury in the ground is the price of redeeming and freeing the wretched.[6]

Ioannes Teutonicus drew this principle of limited rights in property along new lines and attempted to establish juridic

[6] Sed ais: "Quid iniustum est, si cum aliena non invadam, propria diligentius servo?" O impudens dictu! Propria dicis? quae? ex quibus reconditis in hunc mundum detulisti? Quando in hanc ingressus es lucem, quando de ventre matris existi, quibus, quaeso, facultatibus quibusve subsidiis stipatus ingressus es? Proprium nemo dicat, quod est commune, plus quam sufficeret sumptum et violenter obtentum est. . . . Quis enim tam iniustus, tam avarus quam qui multorum alimenta suum non usum, sed (h)abundantiam et delicias facit? . . . Esurientium panis est, quem tu detines; nudoeum indumentum est, quod tu recludis, miserorum redemptio est et absolutio pecunia, quam tu in terra defodis. . . ."—Dist. 47, c. 8. The text originally came from St. Basil and was in Greek. Cf. *MPL,* XVII, col. 613, 614 for St. Ambrose's text. (Translation is the writer's.)

remedies against anyone who did not observe the limits of his rights. Such a remedy was the *denuntiatio evangelica.* In discussing the obligation of the rich to the poor Ioannes Teutonicus cited the Roman law dictum: "It is expedient for the commonwealth [*respublica*] that a man should not use his property badly,"[7] and considered whether a rich man could be juridically compelled to support a particular poor man. The point was a delicate one, because it would be difficult to express such an obligation in quantitative terms, and also because, in lieu of such a remedy, a poor man enjoyed a right which was not legally enforceable. In an attempt at a compromise Ioannes Teutonicus explained that a poor man could denounce before the Church a man who refused to give alms, and the Church could compel him by ecclesiastical censure, not excluding excommunication, to support him. Ioannes admitted, however, that a poor man could not obtain satisfaction "by direct judgment."[8]

In summary, the mediaeval view of private property, although it professed to be based on ancient authorities, a blending of the Church Fathers and Roman law, fitted in very well with contemporary ideas on property holding as exemplified in mediaeval institutions. The mediaeval systems acknowledged individual rights in property, but with corresponding social obligations. The result of canonical thinking was to safeguard the right of private property as such, but at the same time to impose upon the property owner the obligation of supporting the needy.

## SECTION II. THE OWNERSHIP OF CHURCH PROPERTY

The ownership of church property presented special problems to the mediaeval canonists. Previous canonical legislation circum-

[7] *Glossa Ordinaria* ad Dist. 47, c. 8, s.v. *Aliena.*

[8] "Numquid ergo pauperes ipsum possunt petere? Non directo iudicio, sed denuntiare possunt ecclesiae illum qui non dat, et sic ecclesia potest eum cogere ut det. 2."—*Glossa Ordinaria* ad Dist. 47, c. 8, s.v. *denuntiatio.* In a gloss at C. 1, q. 7, c. 18 Ioannes compared a poor man seeking alms with a man seeking a dispensation. At times a dispensation was due, and an ecclesiastical judge would sin if he refused to grant it. If he did refuse, however, there was no legal remedy available to the petitioner. Here again there was place for the *denuntiatio evangelica:* the petitioner would appeal to a superior by "imploring the office of the judge."

scribed the administration of church goods. For instance, a bishop or a priest could not treat church goods as his own; he could not cede them to his family; neither could he bequeath them at will or use them recklessly. In effect, an ecclesiastical person possessed only a limited right over church property. His role was more properly that of a trustee than that of an owner. The larger problem was to determine who did own the property of the Church.

Besides some few attempts to ascribe church property to a particular patron saint, as in some early endowments, the early Church Fathers often spoke of church property as belonging to God in a more special sense than by virtue of its creation.[9] Gratian cited three authors among the early Fathers who held that church property belonged to the poor. St. Augustine (354-430) was quoted as saying: "The things of which we have charge do not belong to us but to the poor."[10] St. Ambrose said: "The Church has gold, not to hoard it away, but to bestow it by way of help to those who are in need."[11] And, finally, St. Jerome (347-420) said: "Whatever clerics have belongs to the poor, and their houses ought to be common to all."[12]

The law also allowed property rights to the clergy (not in vows). For example, Gratian maintained that a cleric could retain ownership of private property but that, if he did so, he could not also obtain his support from the Church.[13] Ioannes Teutonicus disagreed, maintaining that a cleric could own property unless he were under a vow of poverty. On the other hand, Ioannes taught

---

[9] Brian Tierney, *Mediaeval Poor Law* (Berkeley and Los Angeles, California: University of California Press, 1959), p. 40. The author treats the social nature of property in the late Middle Ages with a view that the Church's social institutions responded to the needs of the poor.

[10] "Augustinus ad Bonifacium, comitem, ep. L.: 'Si privatum possidemus, quod nobis sufficiat, non illa nostra sunt, sed pauperum quorum procurationem quodammodo gerimus, non proprietatem nobis usurpatione damnabili vendicamus.' "—c. 28, C. XII, q. 1. Cf. *MPL,* XXXIII, col. 809.

[11] "Aurum ecclesia habet, non ut servet, sed ut eroget, et subveniat in necessitatibus."—c. 70, C. XII, q. 2. Cf. *MPL,* XVI, col. 140.

[12] "Quoniam quidquid habent clerici, pauperum est, et domus illorum omnibus debent esse communes."—c. 68, C. XVI, q. 1.

[13] *Post* c. 24, C. XII, q. 1.

also that a wealthy cleric sinned who avariciously accepted support from the Church.[14] Pope Innocent IV (1243-1254), in a different spirit, held that a priest who was independently wealthy had every right to live "off the altar," that is, from church revenues rather than from his private resources, and this view predominated.[15]

Pope Innocent IV appealed to the doctrine of the Mystical Body of Christ in an attempt to explain how the Church held property and who held it in the name of the Church:

> No prelate, but Christ, has possession and dominion of the things of the Church . . . or the churches have possession, that is to say the community of the faithful which is the body of Christ, the head. They are said to belong to the poor as to sustenance. For the common welfare they are divided among the churches of diverse places by authority of the supreme pontiff, and the administration of them is conceded to bishops and other prelates.[16]

In Pope Innocent's opinion ownership was vested in the whole community, and the poor had a right to support from this common property. Innocent wrote in another place: "The pope and the churches possess all in the name of all men, that thence they may come to the help of all in need."[17] Hostiensis (+ 1271) restated

[14] "Si abundantes de bonis ecclesiae suscipiunt, sive absentes sive praesentes sunt, licet non debet eis denegari portio, quia nemo cogitur suis stipendiis militare, mortaliter tamen peccant, praesertim si ex cupiditate sua reservant." —*Glossa Ordinaria* s.v. Sacrilegium ad c. 6, C. I, q. 2.

[15] "Tamen non credimus quod qui habet beneficium vivere debeat de patrimonio, sed de altari. . . ."—Innocentius IV, *In Quinque Libros Decretalium Commentaria* (Venetiis, 1576), *Commentarium ad Decretalem* 3.5.4, p. 425.

[16] "De hac autem materia potest notari, quod non praelatus, sed Christus dominium et possessionem rerum ecclesiae habet . . . id est aggregatio fidelium quae est corpus Christi capitis . . . Dicuntur etiam esse pauperum quo ad sustentationem, haec autem propter utilitatem communem divisa sunt per ecclesias diversorum locorum summorum pontificum, et episcopis, et aliis praelatis concessa est ministrationeorum."—*Commentarium ad Decretalem* 2.12.4, p. 267. (Translation is the writer's.)

[17] "Nam papa et ecclesiae nomine omnium hominum omnia possident, ut inde omnibus necessitatem habentibus subveniant."—*Commentarium ad Decretalem* 3.34.8, p. 515. (Translation is the writer's.)

and expanded Pope Innocent's arguments. He agreed with Pope Innocent that dominion rested with the *congregatio fidelium,* the community of the faithful, and declared:

> And if at times it is found at law that these [ecclesiastical] goods belong to bishops, or prelates, or the cathedral chapter, it must be understood that these goods belong to them for administrative purposes only, that is, they are actually custodians and not owners. . . . But these goods are said to belong to the poor; and, in this sense, these goods serve for their sustenance . . . because whatever the clergy have under their administration is directed for the sustenance of the poor. And so no one may consider the goods of the Church as his own, but what belongs to the Church is dedicated to the commonweal.[18]

Later on Hostiensis noted that "the pope and churches hold the goods they have not as their own but as common possessions, that thence they may help all men suffering want."[19]

These views which were reflected in the writings of Pope Innocent IV and Hostiensis proved decisive. Later canonists sought not a single owner of the Church's goods, but rather attempted to harmonize the various rights which had some claim over the goods of the Church. This approach corresponded with the actual situation in which the Church found itself in the later Middle Ages, which probably helped not a little toward the attainment

[18] "Et si aliquando inveniatur in iure, quod haec bona sint episcoporum, vel praelatorum, vel capitulorum intellegas quod eorum sunt quo ad gubernationem et administrationem, inde est, quod tales proprie loquendo procuratores et non domini dicuntur . . . sed et haec eadem bona dicuntur esse pauperum, intellegas quo ad sustentationem . . . quoniam quicquid habent clerici quo ad administrationem pauperum est subaudi quo ad sustentationem. Et ideo nullus dicat proprium ecclesiae patrimonium, quod ecclesiae est pro communi utilitate datum."—Henricus Segusio Cardinalis (Hostiensis), *Commentaria in Quinque Libros ad Decretales* (6 vols. in 4, Venetiis, 1581), in lib. 2, tit. 12, c. 4; II, fol. 42 v. (Translation is the writer's.)

[19] "Papa et ecclesiae bona, quae habent et tenent, non tamquam propria, sed tamquam communia possident ut inde omnibus hominibus necessitatem habentibus subveniant."—Hostiensis, *op. cit.,* in 1. 3, tit. 34, c. 48; III, fol. 128 vb. (Translation is the writer's.)

of a viable and juridic solution of the problem. Henricus Boich (+ 1350) summarized the thinking of his contemporaries concerning the ownership of the Church's property:

> If you ask to whom ecclesiastical goods are said to belong, here it is said that they belong to the Church. . . . Elsewhere it is said that they belong to God. . . . Elsewhere it is said that they belong to the poor. . . . And again it is said that they belong to the clergy. . . . But Hostiensis and Ioannes Andreas . . . harmonize the opinions stated above, saying, and I believe rightly, that the Church, that is, the community of the faithful, has dominion over them, and principally Christ as head. What is said of the poor is true as to sustenance, and what is said of the clergy is true as to administration or government, and for this reason clerics are called agents, not owners.[20]

---

[20] "Si quaeris cuius dicantur esse res ecclesiasticae, hic dicitur quod sunt ecclesiae. . . . Alibi dicitur quod bona sunt Dei. . . . Alibi autem dicitur quod sunt pauperum. . . . Et ibidem dicitur quod sunt clericorum. . . . Sed Hostiensis et Ioannes Andreas . . . praedictas opiniones concordant dicendo et bene prout credo quod ecclesia, i.e., congregatio fidelium, habet dominium ipsarum et principaliter Christus tamquam caput. Quod dicuntur pauperum, verum est quo ad sustentationem. Et quod dicuntur clericorum, verum est quo ad administrationem seu gubernationem, et propter hoc clerici dicuntur procuratores non domini." Henricus Boich, *In Quinque Decretalium Libros Commentaria* (Venetiis, 1576), *Distinctiones ad Decretales,* I, 5, tit. 40, c. 13, p. 300. (Translation is the writer's.) It may be noted here that this doctrine reached a curious completion in the thought of John Wyclif. Wyclif held that secular lords possessed a power from God whereby—under the mediaeval concept of one *ecclesia* in which there were two powers: the one secular and the other ecclesiastical—the secular power could remove Church lands or goods from such clerics who, in their judgment, have misused the goods of the Church. Wyclif based his teaching on the doctrine of Giles of Rome and his *De ecclesiastica potestate;* the teaching of William of Cremona and his treatise *Refutatio errorum* against Marsilius of Padua; the disputes among the Franciscans concerning the ideal of poverty; and the influence of John of Gaunt upon him. Cf. L. J. Daly, *The Political Thought of John Wyclif* (Loyola University Press: Chicago, 1962), pp. 56-58; 84-93; 134, 135; 143-151. Cf. also H. B. Workman, "John Wyclif"—*Encyclopaedia of the Social Sciences* (15 vols., ed. by Edwin R. A. Seligman, The Macmillan Company: New York, 1938), Vol. XV, pp. 506, 507.

In summary it may be said that ownership of church property was a problem to the canonists of the later Middle Ages. They recognized the Apostolic communism of the early Christians; yet they admitted the existence of private property rights among themselves. In regard to church property Gratian maintained that a cleric who owned private property could not partake of church property. He was opposed in this view by Ioannes Teutonicus and Pope Innocent IV, who held that a cleric, unless he was in solemn vows, had a right to live "off the altar" independently of his personal financial status, so long as he did not do so with avaricious intent. Hostiensis, attacking the problem on a broader plane, agreed with Pope Innocent IV that the community of the faithful owned church property, and this view prevailed. Every Christian, then, had an interest in the property of the Church: the laity supported the Church and provided its goods; the clergy governed the Church and administered its goods; the poor received their sustenance from the Church. The rights and obligations of every member were mutual, that is, the lay person was obliged to support the Church, the cleric was obliged to administer these ecclesiastical goods according to the law, and the poor were obliged to pray for their benefactors. On the other hand, the laity had a right to the prayers of the poor, the clergy had a right to govern the Church without interference, and the poor had a right to their sustenance.

It was true to say, then, that in this light the right of every ecclesiastic, indeed of every Christian, was a limited one in regard to church property. It was also truc to say that the law restrained the exercise of an ecclesiastic's right over church property and its administration. It is this latter point that will be the subject under consideration in the next section.

## SECTION III. THE LAW OF ALIENATION

Alienation of church property was subject to restrictions in both the previous legislation[21] and in the law of the succeeding cen-

---

[21] The reader is referred to the work of Joseph F. Cleary, *Canonical Limitations on the Alienation of Church Property*, Canon Law Studies, n. 100 (Washington: The Catholic University of America Press, 1936), pp. 39-57, for further treatment on this subject.

turies. Alienation was, indeed, a limitation of the exercise of the right of the disposition of church property, which belonged in some way to the bishop of the diocese. The bishop held this right as trustee of the Church's goods, and not as the owner of them.

There were many aspects of the law of alienation. The law specified by whom church property might be alienated; also to whom and under what circumstances it might be alienated. In the following treatment of the law of alienation as a restraint of the exercise of one's rights, only the prohibition of the law against alienation of church property will be considered.

It has been pointed out that in the previous legislation the power of distributing the belongings of the Church as the need arose lay with the bishop of the diocese.[22] This power was not to be used indiscriminately, however,[23] and was restricted in many respects. The bishop was prohibited from alienating valuable real estate pertaining to the Church.[24] He was not to lease perpetually by *emphyteusis* any property upon which a church depended for its support, nor could he dispose of any country estates, or otherwise jeopardize their condition, whether the alienation were made to a prince of the nation or not.[25] Any such contract was invalid.[26] Finally, a bishop, during the term of his episcopacy, or a priest, during his pastorate, could not alienate property which had been acquired during his term of office.[27]

Pope Gregory IX (1227-1241) promulgated his Decretals in 1234. He included the basic definitions of Justinian in the *Corpus Iuris Civilis* on the topic of alienation,[28] namely, that alienation comprised any sale, donation, exchange, or perpetual contract of *emphyteusis*, and that no one was to be permitted to alienate the immovable property of the Church, whether buildings or land, or burden it with a special mortgage, under pain of the penalties

---

[22] *Supra*, pp. 36, 37; cf. also c. 7, C. X, q. 2; cc. 51, 53, C. XII, q. 2.

[23] C. 18, C. XII, q. 2.

[24] C. 20, C. XII, q. 2.

[25] *Ibid.*, c. 13.

[26] *Ibid.*, c. 19.

[27] *Ibid.*, c. 12; cf. also c. 52 (Dictum Gratiani).

[28] C.(1.2)14; Nov. VII, 1.

of the Leonine Constitution.[29] The bishop could not alienate the property of the *mensa episcopalis* or of the cathedral chapter. All unlawful alienations were to be revoked.[30]

The *Liber Sextus* of Pope Boniface VIII (1294-1303) contained a decretal invalidating the alienation of church property without a just cause, even though the legal formalities were duly observed.[31]

Pope Clement V (1305-1314) included a canon from the Council of Vienne in his collection of decretals to the effect that any cleric who alienated for life or for a long period of time the possessions which he administered, unless a just cause permitted or necessitated the alienation, incurred suspension from office, and the alienation was rendered invalid.[32]

A Synod of Exeter which was held in 1287 declared invalid any alienation of church property, whether by sale, donation, exchange, lease of perpetual *emphyteusis,* or pledge, by any cleric of whatever status. Excommunication was threatened unless restitution was made.[33] Also it had been forbidden to alienate churches or ecclesiastical benefices.[34] In order to contravene the practice in England of giving church goods in pledge without redeeming them, consent was required from the bishop in every case; otherwise the alienation was void.[35]

---

[29] C. 5, X, *de rebus ecclesiae alienandis vel non,* III, 13. *Decretales D. Gregorii Papae IX, suae integritati una cum glossis restitutae, cum privilegio Gregorii XIII, Pont. Max., et Aliorum Principum* (Romae, 1582).

[30] *Ibid.,* c. 10; cf. Pope Innocent III (1198-1216), *Epistolae,* 1, I, nn. 105, 106 (1198)—*MPL,* CCXIV, col. 92, 93.

[31] C. 1, *de rebus ecclesiae non alienandis,* III, 9, in VI°. *Liber Sextus Decretalium D. Bonifatii Papae VIII suae integritati cum Clementinis Extravagantibus, earumque Glossis restitutis* (Romae, 1582).

[32] C. 1, *de rebus ecclesiae non alienandis,* III, 4, in Clem. *Liber Sextus Decretalium D. Bonifatii Papae VIII Clementis Papae V Constitutiones, Extravagantes tum Viginti D. Ioannis Papae XXII, tum communes, haec omnia cum suis glossis suae integritati restituta et ad exemplar Romanum diligenter recognita* (Taurinae, 1588).

[33] Synod of Exeter (1287), canon 26—Hardouin, VII, 1100; Mansi, XXIV, 814.

[34] Council of London (1127), canon 1—Hardouin, VI, 1130; Mansi, XXI, 355.

[35] Council of Lambeth (1330), canon 7—Hardouin, VII, 1554; Constitutions of Bishop Richard Poore (1217), caput 41—Hardouin, VII, 101; Mansi, XXII, 1121.

The national Council of Würzburg (1287) legislated against the prevalent abuse of transferring church property to relations and friends of the clergy. Those who presumed to do so were excommunicated; the contracts of transfer were void; and the guilty clergy were held to make restitution.[36]

The same abuses prevailed in Austria. The Council of Salzburg (1281) legislated that needless alienations made without the consent of the bishop were void. The cleric who alienated the property was suspended until restitution was made.[37]

The Hungarian national synod held at Ofen (Buda) in 1279 declared that no prelate was to alienate church property without a just reason and without the consent of his proper superior.[38] The provisions of this council included all kinds of property, all classes of persons, and every kind of alienation under these provisions.[39]

Abuses of alienation whereby prelates administering church property transferred it to lay persons, either temporarily or permanently, for almost any reason were prohibited in Spain.[40] As a result, no one, no matter what his condition or status, was allowed to alienate church property in any way; and any such attempts were null and void in law.[41]

The Council of Constance in 1418, which became an ecumenical council in its later sessions—sessions 41 to 45—defined in canon 9 of its forty-third session, after repeating the necessity of consent for the validity of alienation, that the consent of the council, together with approval of a majority of the cardinals was necessary

---

[36] Canon 9—Hardouin, VII, 1134, 1135; Mansi, XXIV, 854; cf. also Synod of Cologne (1280), canon 12—Hardouin, VII, 831; Mansi, XXIV, 358.

[37] Council of Salzburg, canon 1—Hardouin, VII, 855, 856; Mansi, XXIV, 397.

[38] Council of Buda, canon 29—Hardouin, VII, 799; Mansi, XXIV, 284.

[39] Canon 50—Hardouin, VII, 805; Mansi, XXIV, 293.

[40] Council of Palencia, Province of Castille (1388), canon 4—Hardouin, VII, 1910.

[41] Council of Toledo (1339), canon 1—Hardouin, VII, 1637; Mansi, XXV, 1144. Cf. Council of Melfi (1284), canon 7—Mansi, XXIV, 574 and the Council of Palermo (1388)—Mansi, XXVI, 751.

for the leasing of all vicariates, lands, cities, and dominions for a period beyond five years.[42]

Pope Paul II (1464-1471), in order to curtail the abuse of unnecessary acts of alienation of church property, issued the constitution *Ambitiosae* on March 1, 1467, which prohibited the alienation of immovable property or of movable property of considerable value. The Constitution stated in part:

> If, in opposition to the prohibitions herein mentioned, anyone should presume to alienate any goods or estate of the Church either by absolute alienation, mortgage, grant, rental or enfeoffment, such an act lacks all force and is null and void. Moreover, both the one who alienates the property and the one who receives the property thus alienated incur a sentence of excommunication.[43]

The constitution *Ambitiosae* was the last piece of major legislation concerning the alienation of church property before the Council of Trent (1545-1563). Together with the preceding conciliar legislation and decretal law it provided a continuing reassertion of the Church's legal power of restraining the free exercise of the rights of its members under conditions which it judged disadvantageous to the common good of its members. The same orientation was to continue up to the present Code of Canon Law.

---

[42] Council of Constance, Sess. XLIII, canon 9—Hardouin, VIII, 880.

[43] "Si quis autem contra huius nostrae prohibitionis seriem de bonis et rebus eisdem quicquam alienare praesumpserit: alienatio, hypotheca, concessio, locatio, conductio et infeudatio huiusmodi, nullius omnino sint roboris vel momenti, et tam qui alienat, quam is, qui alienatas res et bona praedicta receperit, sententiam excommunicationis incurrat. . . ."—C. un., *de rebus ecclesiae non alienandis,* III, 4, in Extravag. Com. (Translation is the writer's.) *Extravagantes Decretales, quae a diversis Romanis Pontificibus Post Sextum, emanaverunt Quarum aliquae Glossis Ioannis Monachi Picardi Cardinalis, aliquae commentariis Guglielmi de Monte Lauduno, et Ioannis Francisci de Paomis illustrantur.*

# CHAPTER IV

## The Right of Ownership From the Council of Trent Until the Code of Canon Law

### SECTION I. THE LAW OF ALIENATION

The importance of the constitution *Ambitiosae* may be seen from its incorporation into subsequent church legislation. The Council of Trent (1545-1563) undertook to restate the doctrine and discipline of the Catholic Church in order to counteract the spread of the classical heresies (Lutheranism, Zwinglianism, Calvinism, Wesleyanism, etc.), and attain a reformation within the Church. In such a broad program of reform the Church saw little need to add to the already existing restrictions concerning the law of alienation of church property. Instead, the Fathers of the Council contented themselves with enacting a decree to the effect that no renting of church property was to be considered valid which was prejudicial to the rights of the successor to a benefice, any privilege or indult to the contrary notwithstanding.[1] Cardinal Pole (1500-1558) inserted a decree into the acts of the Council which applied the provisions of the constitution *Ambitiosae* to the Church in England.[2] The constitutions of several succeeding popes renewed the dispositions of the constitution *Ambitiosae* in the continuing struggle against abuses.[3]

---

[1] Concilium Tridentinum, sessio XXV, *de reformatione,* c. 11—Mansi, XXXIII, 188-189; Hardouin, X, 185.

[2] Conc. Trid., Decretum X (*de reformatione Angliae*—1556)—Hardouin, X, 407.

[3] Paulus IV (1555-1559), const. *Iniunctum nobis,* 14 iul., 1555—*Codicis Iuris Canonici Fontes,* cura Emi Petri Gasparri editi (9 vols., Romae [postea Civitate Vaticana]: Typis Polyglottis Vaticanis, 1923-1939; Vols. VII-IX, ed. cura et studio Emi Iustiniani Card. Serédi), n. 88 [hereafter cited as *Fontes*]; Pius V (1566-1572), const. *Admonet nos,* 29 mart., 1567—*Fontes,* n. 120; Gregorius XIII (1572-1585), const. *Inter caetera,* 26 maii, 1572—*Fontes,* n. 142; Sixtus V (1585-1590), const. *Quanta Apostolicae,* 18 mart., 1586—*Fontes,* n. 158; Gregorius XIV, const. *Romanus pontifex,*

Just as the constitution *Ambitiosae* received additional emphasis from the decrees of the popes, so it also found its way into particular conciliar legislation. The II Provincial Council of Milan, held in 1569, incorporated the provisions of the Constitution among its canons.[4] The Council of Malines (1570)[5] in Belgium and the Council of Tours (1583)[6] in France added further precisions to the general legislation of the constitution of Pope Paul II. The *Ambitiosae* was almost contained verbatim in the Provincial Council of Mexico (1585), which reflected the influence of the Council of Trent as well as the Spanish councils.[7] The constitution *Ambitiosae* served as the basis of conciliar legislation in Italy for the law of alienation.[8]

The Council of Utrecht (1865) in Holland incorporated the *Ambitiosae* into its statutes.[9] It placed special emphasis on sacred vestments and vessels as well as paintings and statues. They were not to be alienated without a just cause.[10]

---

19 dec., 1590—*Fontes,* n. 168; Innocentius IX (1591), const. *Quae ab hac,* 4 nov., 1591—*Fontes,* n. 174; Clemens VIII (1592-1605), const. *Ad Romani,* 14 febr., 1592—*Fontes,* n. 175; Paulus V (1605-1621), const. *Inter caetera,* 30 dec., 1605—*Fontes,* n. 193; Urbanus VIII (1623-1644), const. *Sacrosancti,* 30 sept., 1623—*Fontes,* n. 203.

[4] II Council of Milan, tit. III, decret. 5-11—Hardouin, X, 750-752.

[5] Canons 1, 2—Mansi, XXXIV, 577; Hardouin, X, 1171.

[6] Canon 20—Hardouin, X, 1436, 1437.

[7] Lib. III, tit. 8 (II, III)—Hardouin, X, 1676; Mansi, XXXIV, 1110-1112.

[8] Cf. Council of Benevento (1693), cap. un., tit. 23—*Collectio Lacensis, Acta et Decreta Sacrorum Conciliorum Recentiorum* (7 vols., Friburgi Brisgoviae, 1870-1892), I, 52 (hereafter cited as *Coll. Lac.*); Council of Rome (1725), cap. un., tit. 19, I (II, III)—*Coll. Lac.*, I, 380, 381; Council of Naples (1699), cap. un., tit. 13 (10)—*Coll. Lac.*, I, 241; National Synod of Albano (1703), Pars IV, canon 2—*Coll. Lac.*, I, 327; Brief of Pope Benedict XIII (1724-1730) to the city and diocese of Benevento (1724)—*Coll. Lac.*, I, 441, 442. The Oriental rites followed the same legislation. Cf. Provincial Synod of the Ruthenians (Greek Uniate Rite) at Zamość (Poland) in 1720, c. 13—*Coll. Lac.*, II, 59; Maronite Synod of Mount Lebanon (1736), Pars IV, c. 1, nn. 12-14—*Coll. Lac.*, II, 352, 353; *ibid.*, c. 2, n. 3—*Coll. Lac.*, II, 357; Armenian Council in Bzommar (Cilicia, Asia Minor—1866)—*Coll. Lac.*, II, 572, 576; Apostolic Letters of Pius IX to the Fathers of the Council of Bzommar; letter I and letter II, n. 7—*loc. cit.*

[9] Ti. X, c. 1—*Coll. Lac.*, V, 922, 923.

[10] Tit. X, c. 3—*Coll. Lac.*, V, 925.

The Council of Lyons (1850) in France recalled the common law concerning alienation in its statutes.[11]

The II Provincial Council of Westminster (1855) in England stated that there had to be some necessity for the alienation of church property before such alienation could become admissible in law. Certain conditions had to be fulfilled before the bishop could allow the alienation.[12]

The II Provincial Council of Quebec (1854) in Canada forbade administrators of church property to give, sell, exchange, or in any other way alienate church properties, whether movable or immovable, give in loan, in lease or *emphyteusis,* or in mortgage, without first having consulted the bishop and obtained his express permission, except in the cases allowed by the common law.[13]

No mention is made of alienation of church property in the I Plenary Council of Baltimore (1852), but the II Plenary Council of Baltimore (1866) warned priests of the United States not to contract debts rashly for the building or repairing of churches, etc., or to borrow money without the permission of the bishop.[14]

The III Plenary Council of Baltimore (1884) relaxed some of the provisions of the II Plenary Council because of the difficulty of contact with Rome on the part of the Church in the United States.[15] This was the situation in which the Church in the United States found itself when the Code of Canon Law was promulgated in 1917.

One can hardly escape the conclusion that the constitution *Ambitiosae* influenced the legislation of the Church after the Council of Trent. Likewise, it is true that these laws restrained the right of alienation of church property on the part of the administrators of the Church's goods. It is equally undeniable that, to the extent that the administrators of the goods of the Church possessed the right of disposition as well as the use and enjoy-

---

[11] Decret. 23, n. 7—*Coll. Lac.,* IV, 482.

[12] Decret. 8, n. 8—*Coll. Lac.,* III, 981.

[13] Decret. 15, § 2, n. 4—*Coll. Lac.,* III, 657.

[14] *Acta et Decreta Concilii Plenarii Baltimorensis* II (1866) (Baltimorae, 1894), n. 192—*Coll. Lac.,* III, 89.

[15] *Acta et Decreta Concilii Plenarii Baltimorensis* III (1884) (Baltimorae, 1886), p. ciii, and n. 20, 6°.

ment of those same goods for the benefit of the Church, such a law of alienation constituted a legal restraint of the exercise of their (the administrators') rights.

## SECTION II. SOURCE OF THE LAW OF THE CODE

The Code of Canon Law, which was promulgated in 1917 and became the common law of the Church in 1918, states in canon 19:

> Laws which establish a penalty, restrict the free exercise of rights, or contain an exception to the law are to be strictly interpreted.[16]

Van Hove (1872-1947) in his commentary on canon 19 noted that this formula was new to the Code of Canon Law,[17] and that it was taken from Italian Civil Law.[18] Van Hove also pointed out that the Italian law was meant to restrict an interpretation of law from case to case, whereas canon 19 speaks of a strict interpretation of law. The matter of each law is, in Van Hove's words: ". . . very much interconnected."[19]

One may conclude, then, that those rights which were recognized in law and were protected in law also suffered some legal restrictions when these restrictions seemed necessary for the common good or the general welfare of the subjects of the law. This was equally true of Roman Law, of Germanic Law, and of Canon Law in their development. The right of private property provides a representative example of these restrictions, because private property pertains, as a right, to the natural law and has,

---

[16] "Leges quae poenam statuunt, aut liberum iurium exercitium coarctant, aut exceptionem a lege continent, strictae subsunt interpretationi." (Translation is the writer's.)

[17] Alphonsus Van Hove, *Commentarium Lovaniense in Codicem Iuris Canonici* (1 vol. in 5 tomes, Tome I, *Prolegomena,* 2. ed., 1945; Tome II, *De Legibus Ecclesiasticis,* Romae: Dessain, 1930), II, n. 298.

[18] "Le leggi penali e quelle che restringono il libero esercizio dei diritti o formano eccezione alle regole generali o ad altre leggi, non si estendono oltre i casi e tempi in esse espressi."—Italian Civil Code, Article IV (1865), as quoted by Van Hove, *loc. cit.*

[19] "Materiae tamen utriusque dispositionis sunt valde connexae."—*Loc. cit.*

as a matter of fact, been subject to the most diverse and most numerous restrictions in the course of Western Christian civilization. It is also true, however, that the restraint of the exercise of one's rights, of which the right of property was but an example, did not attain separate status as an institute of law until almost the beginning of the Twentieth Century. It would seem, then, that such a continuing growth within the framework of fundamental legal concepts bodes well for the spread of a rule of law in a world which is desperately in need of proof of its philosophical and legal bases.

# PART TWO

## Canonical Commentary

# CHAPTER V

## The Theological and Philosophical Foundations of Freedom and Its Restraint

### SECTION I. THE THEOLOGICAL FOUNDATIONS OF FREEDOM AND ITS RESTRAINT

### *Article 1. Magisterium of the Church*

#### A. Freedom of the Will

The Church has constantly taught that freedom of the human will is an essential element of the divine economy. Man is considered by the Church as a free being who is responsible for his actions, as a being who achieves his spiritual destiny—under the inspiration of grace—by his own choice. A sketch of the historical teaching of the Church regarding freedom of the will may help toward gaining an understanding of the limitation of freedom as a function of the common good and man's last end, which is the vision of God.

In the early Church shortly after the reign of St. Celestine I (422-432), there was issued an *"Indiculus" de gratia Dei,* which affirmed the existence of free will while treating of man's native inability to regain justification after the fall of Adam.[1] In the pontificate of St. Felix III (526-530) the II Council of Orange (529) in the course of answering the Pelagian heresy that only man's body was touched by original sin, and not his soul, also stated the Christian doctrine of free will.[2] During the pontificate of St. Leo IV (847-855) the Council of Quierzy (853) asserted

[1] ". . . per liberum arbitrium . . . suaque in aeternum libertate deceptus; . . . Quod nemo, nisi per Christum, libero bene utatur arbitrio; . . ."—Henricus Denzinger, *Enchiridion Symbolorum, definitionum et declarationum de rebus fidei et morum,* quod post Clementem Bannwart et Ioannem B. Umberg, S.I., denuo edidit Carolus Rahner, S.I. (editio 31, Friburgi Brisgoviae: Herder, 1957), nn. 130, 133 (hereafter cited as Denz.).

[2] Denz., nn. 174, 180, 186; *MGH,* III, *Concilia,* T.I., 46 ff.; Mansi, VIII, 712.

man's freedom against Gottschalk and the Predestinationists.[3]

In the late Middle Ages St. Leo IX (1049-1054) sent a letter of congratulations to Bishop Peter of Antioch on April 13, 1053, which contained a *Symbolum Fidei* in which the new bishop subscribed to man's freedom as an article of faith.[4] The same doctrine was reaffirmed in the pontificate of Innocent II (1130-1143) at the Council of Sens (1140-1141) in the condemnation of the errors of Peter Abelard.[5] Pope Leo X (1513-1521) in the Bull *Exsurge, Domine* of June 15, 1520, condemned the errors of Martin Luther, who held that free will existed only potentially in man after the sin of Adam.[6] The condemnation of the errors of Martin Luther was the last statement by the Church on the existence of free will before the Council of Trent (1545-1563), which reaffirmed the foundations of Catholic doctrine.

The Council of Trent was convoked by Pope Paul III (1543-1549) and at the end of its Sixth Session it issued the decree on Justification on January 13, 1547. In chapters one and five of this decree the Council treated respectively of the inability of the human spirit to attain justification by its own powers and of the absolute gratuity of supernatural grace from God as a means of salvation.[7] The doctrine contained in these two chapters as it

[3] "Cap. 1. Deus omnipotens hominem sine peccato rectum cum libero arbitrio condidit. . . ."—Denz., n. 316; Mansi, XIV, 920: Hardouin, V, 18C; *MPL*, XLIX, col. 129 ff. Cf. also Denz., nn. 317, 322, 325.

[4] ". . . liberum arbitrium rationali creaturae non denegem. . . ."—ep. *Congratulamur vehementer;* cf. Philippus Jaffé, *Regesta Pontificum Romanorum,* ab condita ecclesia ad annum post Christum natum MCXCVIII (2. ed., 2 vols., correctam et auctam auspiciis Gulielmi Wattenbach curaverunt F. Kaltenbrunner ad annum 590, P. Ewald ab anno 590 ad annum 882, S. Loewenfeld ab anno 882 ad annum 1198, Lipsiae, 1885-1888), JE, n. 4297; *MPL,* CXLIII, col. 771; Hardouin, VI, I, 954; Mansi, XIX, 663; Denz., n. 348.

[5] "Quod liberum arbitrium per se sufficit ad aliquod bonum." (Condemned proposition)—Denz., n. 373; Mansi, XXI, 568; Hardouin, VI, II, 1224 (proposition not included in Hardouin).

[6] "Liberum arbitrium post peccatum est res de solo titulo; et dum facit, quod in se est, peccat mortaliter." (Condemned proposition)—Denz., n. 776; Mansi, XXXII, 1053; Hardouin, IX, 1894.

[7] Denz., nn. 793, 797; Concilium Tridentinum, sessio VI, *de iustificatione;* Mansi, XXXIII, 33, 34; Hardouin, X, 33, 34.

pertained to free will appeared in canon 5, which was appended to the same decree as a condemnation of the Lutheran teaching.[8]

From the Council of Trent until the Encyclical *Libertas praestantissimum* of Pope Leo XIII (1878-1903) the Church was mainly concerned with the defense of the doctrine of free will against individual heretics. Shortly after the Council of Trent St. Pius V (1566-1572) condemned the errors of Michael de Bay in the Bull *Ex omnibus afflictionibus* which was issued on October 1, 1567.[9] Bay (Baius) had held after the Pelagians that free will, without the aid of grace, cannot avoid sinning. Similarly Pope Innocent X (1644-1655) condemned the five propositions of Cornelius Jansenius (1585-1638) who held that the will was not free in either the reception of grace or the commission of sin.[10] In the same spirit Pope Alexander VIII (1689-1691), in a decree of the Holy Office of December 7, 1690, condemned similar errors of the Jansenists.[11]

In the eighteenth century Pope Clement XI (1700-1721) condemned the errors of E. Paschasius Quesnel (1634-1719) in the dogmatic constitution *Unigenitus* of September 8, 1713.[12] Quesnel had taught that grace could not be impeded or retarded because it represented the activity of an omnipotent God. In the nineteenth century Pope Pius IX (1846-1878) condemned the teaching of Augustine Bonnetty (1798-1879) in a decree issued by the Sacred Congregation of the Index on June 11, 1855.[13] Pope Leo XIII (1878-1903) condemned the doctrine of E. Antonio de Rosmini-Serbati (1797-1855) in a decree of the Holy Office,

---

[8] "Si quis liberum hominis arbitrium post Adae peccatum amissum et exstinctum esse dixerit, aut rem esse de solo titulo, immo titulo sine re, figmentum denique a satana invectum in Ecclesiam, A.S."—Denz., n. 815; Mansi, XXXIII, 40; Hardouin, X, 40. Cf. also *supra*, footnote 6, for the condemned proposition.

[9] Denz., nn. 1027, 1028, 1041.

[10] Denz., nn. 1092-1096.

[11] Denz., n. 1291.

[12] Denz., n. 1360.

[13] "Ratiocinatio . . . hominis libertatem cum certitudine probare potest. . . ."—*Acta Sanctae Sedis* (41 vols., Romae, 1865-1908), III (1867), 224 (hereafter cited as *ASS*); Denz., n. 1650.

which was given on December 14, 1887.[14] Rosmini had held that the union of soul and body consisted in an immanent perception whereby the subject intuiting an idea affirms something sensible, and only after this sensible affirmation does the subject intuit the essence of an idea. Rosmini thereby effectively denied the spiritual power of understanding of man; and as a consequence he likewise denied the presence or effectiveness of a rational appetite in man. Pope Leo XIII also issued an encyclical *Libertas praestantissimum* on June 20, 1888, in which he described human liberty as "the highest of natural endowments, being the portion only of intellectual or rational creatures."[15]

Pope John XXIII (1958-1963) issued his encyclical *Pacem in Terris* on April 11, 1963, which included this statement on the freedom of man:

> Any human society if it is to be well-ordered and productive, must lay down as a foundation this principle, namely, that every human being is a person, that is, his nature is endowed with intelligence and free will. Indeed, precisely because he is a person he has rights and obligations flowing directly and simultaneously from his very nature.[16]

### B. Restraint of Freedom

There are times when man's natural and moral freedom—natural because of man's ability to choose or not to choose, and moral because of his ability to choose between good and evil—is subjected to some limitation. In his encyclical *Libertas praestantis-*

---

[14] *ASS,* XX (1887), 403, 404; cf. also XXI (1888), 709; Denz., nn. 1912, 1994.

[15] *ASS,* XX (1887), 593.

[16] "Porro in quovis humano convictu, quem bene compositum et commodum esse velimus, illud principium pro fundamento ponendum est, omnem hominem personae induere proprietatem; hoc est, naturam esse, intelligentia et voluntatis libertate praeditam; atque ideo, ipsum per se iura et officia habere, a sua ipsius natura directo et una simul profluentia."—*AAS,* LV (1963), 259. Cf. Radio Message of Pius XII, Christmas Eve, 1942, *AAS.* XXXV (1943), 9-24; Discourse of John XXIII, January 4, 1963, *AAS,* LV (1963), 89-91.

*simam*[17] Pope Leo XIII declared that freedom of worship,[18] of speech, and of conscience are not absolute freedoms, but may at times be restrained for the common good. The same pontiff in his encyclical *Quod Apostolici Muneris* of December 28, 1878,[19] warned that citizens may have to endure infringement of their freedom by tyrannical governments because the Church generally does not allow rebellion by private authority against such a government, lest public order suffer more because of the rebellion, and society take greater hurt from it.

On the subject of the relationship of private property and poverty Pope Leo XIII taught in the same document that "The (Church) is constantly pressing on the rich that most grave precept to give what remains (of their abundance) to the poor; and it holds over their heads the divine sentence that unless they succor the needy they will be repaid by eternal torments."[20] In his encyclical *Rerum Novarum* of May 15, 1891,[21] Pope Leo XIII taught that "the right to possess private property is derived from nature, not from man; and the State has the right to control its use in the interests of the public good alone, but by no means to absorb it altogether."[22] This same thought was expressed by Pope Pius XI (1922-1939) in his encyclical *Quadragesimo Anno* of May 15, 1931,[23] when he praised those who "seek to define

---

[17] *ASS,* XX (1887), pp. 603-609.

[18] Pope Leo was considering this matter from the speculative viewpoint. Pope Pius XII (1939-1958) adhered to the same doctrine but outlined practical norms which would allow the tolerance of divergence of worship for the common good. Cf. Address to the Fifth Convention of Italian Catholic Jurists, December 6, 1953—T. L. Bouscaren, *The Canon Law Digest* (5 vols., Milwaukee: Bruce and Company, 1934-1964), IV, 3-9; *Acta Apostolicae Sedis* (Romae, 1909- ), XLV (1953), 802 (hereafter cited as *AAS*).

[19] *ASS,* XI (1878), 872 ff.; Denz., 1850.

[20] Denz., n. 1852; translation basically as edited by Etienne Gilson in *The Church Speaks to the Modern World* (Garden City, N. Y.: Doubleday and Co., 1954), p. 196.

[21] *ASS,* XXIII (1890-1891), 641 ff.; Denz., n. 1938b.

[22] Gilson, *The Church Speaks to the Modern World,* p. 231.

[23] *AAS,* XXIII (1931), 192, 193; English translation taken from *The Church and the Reconstruction of the Modern World* (edited by Terence P. McLaughlin, Garden City, N. Y.: Doubleday and Co., 1957), p. 235.

the inner nature of these duties and their limits (that is, duties and limits inherent in ownership) whereby either the right of property or its use, that is, the exercise of ownership, is circumscribed by the necessities of social living."

Pope John XXIII endorsed this teaching by implication when, speaking of the interdependence of the rights and obligations of individuals, he said:

> One of the fundamental duties of civil authorities, therefore, is to coordinate social relations in such a fashion that the exercise of one man's rights does not threaten others in the exercise of their own rights nor hinder them in the fulfillment of their duties. Finally, the rights of all should be effectively safeguarded and, if they have been violated, completely restored.[24]

### *Article 2. Sacred Scripture*

#### A. Freedom of the Will

The idea of freedom is used in several senses in Sacred Scripture. Sometimes freedom may signify a cessation of slavery; and then freemen are set against bondsmen as one category is set against its opposite.[25] In other contexts, in the New Testament, freedom may mean a freedom from Mosaic legal observances for Christians. At one time St. Paul speaks of false brethren who followed him so as to "spy on the liberty" which he enjoyed as

---

[24] "Praeterea ii qui reipublicae gubernacula tractant in praecipuo officio sunt apte convenienterque iura, quibus homines alii cum aliis societate coniunguntur, ita componere et moderari, ne primum cives iura sua persequentes, alteros in suis iuribus interpellent; ne deinde alius sua servans iura, alios officia sua obeuntes retardet; ut postremo omnium iura cum efficaciter sarta tecta conserventur, tum in integrum, si quae violata sint, restituantur." —*AAS,* LV (1963), 274. Cf. also *AAS,* XXIX (1937), 81; XXXV (1943), 9-24.

[25] Examples of freedom-slavery opposition are to be found in Lev. 19:20; Deut. 15:12; Jer. 34:8, 15, 17; Isaiah, 61:1. The reader is referred to the article "Liberté" in the *Dictionnaire de la Bible* (edited by F. Vigouroux, 5 vols., Paris, 1912), II, col. 237, 238 for a more expansive treatment of this subject. Cf. also "Freedom" in the *Dictionary of the Bible* (edited by James Hastings (4 vols., New York, 1900), II, 66.

a Christian.[26] At another time St. Paul refers to his freedom from the Mosaic Law in a reference to meat previously offered to idols: "There is no reason why I should let my freedom be called in question by another man's conscience. I can eat such food and be grateful for it; why should I incur reproach for saying grace over it?"[27] A similar statement is made by St. Peter as regards the relationship of Christian freedom and observance of the Mosaic Law.[28] Freedom is also used in reference to moral choice in Sacred Scripture. It is this sense of that word that is relevant to this presentation.

Moral freedom, that is, the ability to choose between good and evil is never specifically named in Scripture. The reason for this lack of terminology lies largely in that characteristic of the Semitic mind which abhorred abstraction and emphasized concrete images.[29] It must be said, however, that free will is always supposed in the Bible and that man is responsible for his actions.[30] This responsibility is observable in the moral code of the Jewish nation. For example, adultery is considered sinful,[31] as is also the abuse of one's marriage rights.[32] It is related in the Bible that Jacob realized that his deception of Isaac, his father, and Esau, his brother, merited "a curse, not a blessing."[33] even though he followed the advice of his mother, Rebecca. It is also recounted that Judah knew he had done wrong when he withheld his son Sela from marrying Thamar.[34] The Lord also asked Cain: "If thy actions are good, canst thou doubt they will be rewarded?"[35]

---

[26] Gal. 2:4. Similar references are found in the same epistle at 4:26; 5:1 and 13. [Note: All quotations from the Bible are taken from Rt. Rev. Msgr. Ronald A. Knox's translation (New York: Sheed and Ward, 1956).]

[27] I Cor. 10:29, 30.

[28] I Peter 2:16.

[29] *A Catholic Commentary on Holy Scripture* (edited by Dom Bernard Orchard, Edmund F. Sutcliffe, Reginald C. Fuller, Ralph Russell, New York: Thomas Nelson, 1953), n. 19 h.

[30] *Dictionnaire de la Bible,* "art. cit."

[31] Gen. 12:17; 20:3; 39:9.

[32] Gen. 38:9.

[33] Gen. 27:12.

[34] Gen. 38:26.

[35] Gen. 4:7.

And again Moses tells the Jewish people of their duties to God upon promulgating the covenant.

> See I have set before thee this day a choice between life and death, between good fortune and ill. Thou art to love the Lord Thy God and follow the path he has chosen for thee, to hold fast by all his commandments and observances and decrees, if thou wouldst thrive and prosper through him in the land that is to be thy home. If thy heart becomes estranged from him, so that thou dost no longer obey him, but art tempted away into worshipping other gods and doing them service, then I warn thee here and now that it will be thy ruin.[36]

This idea of moral freedom and consequent personal responsibility was re-emphasized in the Book of Ezechiel.[37]

### B. Restraint of Freedom

It must be said that, although the *magisterium* of the Church and the constant teaching of the Fathers emphasize the freedom of man as an element of his nature, it is only in Sacred Scripture that one finds an express mention of the restraint of the exercise of one's freedom as an operable procedure of the Christian life.

The idea of the restraint of freedom is exemplified in the decree of the Council of Jerusalem. The occasion of the Council and its decree was a dispute concerning the observance of the Mosaic Law by Gentile Christians in Antioch. Behind this dispute lay a belief among some Christian Pharisees that the Gentile converts "cannot be saved without being circumcised according to the tradition of Moses."[38] Since this confrontation of Jewish and Gentile Christian was to be the first of many in the future—the decree is also addressed to the Churches of Syria and Cilicia—it became the precedent for Gentile-Jewish relations in the newly

---

[36] Gen. 30:15-18.

[37] Ch. 18:1-32. The point of the chapter is pithily expressed in verse 4: "It is the guilty soul that must die." This verse is repeated in verse 20 of the same chapter. The positive emphasis is given in verse 21, where repentance is allowed as a means of avoiding death.

[38] Acts 15:1.

formed Church. It was only logical that the partisans of both opinions, Paul and Barnabas opposed by the Christian Pharisees, brought the dispute to the Church at Jerusalem. In the presence of Peter and James the divergent opinions were argued by their respective proponents.[39] Peter agreed with Paul as a matter of principle that Gentile Christians were not bound by the Mosaic Law, although Paul was later to take Peter to task for not practicing what he preached because he feared the reaction of the Jewish Christians.[40]

In an earlier chapter of the *Acts of the Apostles*[41]. Peter had received a vision from God concerning the mixture of clean and unclean foods, and the divine command to baptize the pagan Cornelius as indications of the cessation of the Mosaic Law. It was admitted by Peter, Paul and James, therefore, that Gentile Christians were free from observing the Mosaic Law, and could not be forced to observe the law as bound to it. It was also admitted, furthermore, that Gentile Christians were equal in all religious matters to the Jewish converts. Nevertheless, in spite of this freedom from the Mosaic Law, the three Apostles imposed four restrictions from the Mosaic Law upon the Gentile Christians[42] by virtue of their apostolic authority in order to render

---

[39] Acts 15:3-12.

[40] Gal. 2:11-14.

[41] Cf. 11:1-18.

[42] "The first three (restrictions) were included substantially in the seven precepts of the sons of Noah ('Noachic precepts'), which, according to rabbinic legislation had to be observed by non-Israelites living in Israelitic territory (*Sanhedrin*, 56 b). The meat of sacrificial animals was abominable because it was believed that in eating it one participated as it were in the idolatrous sacrifice in which it had been offered. Blood or the meat of animals not previously bled was abominated because of the very ancient belief among Semitic people—accepted by the Mosaic Law (cf. Gen. 9:3, 4; Lev. 17:10-14)—that the blood was the seat of the soul, and by eating it, therefore, one absorbed the soul of the animal with all its brutish qualities."—Giuseppe Riccotti, *Paul the Apostle*, translated by Alba I. Zizzamia (Milwaukee: Bruce, 1953), n. 360. The restriction from fornication probably refers to marriage with blood-relatives, which was forbidden by the law. Cf. Ferdinand Prat, *The Theology of Saint Paul*, translated by John L. Stoddard (2 vols., Westminster, Md.: 1926), I, 49.

social and stable relations possible between two different groups of Christians. The decree speaks for itself:

> To the Gentile brethren in Antioch, Syria and Cilicia, their brethren the apostles and presbyters send greeting. We hear that some of our number who visited you have disquieted you by what they said, unsettling your consciences; although we had given them no commission; and therefore, meeting together with common purpose of heart, we have resolved to send you chosen messengers (Judas and Silas), in company with our well-beloved Barnabas and Paul, men who have staked their lives for the name of our Lord Jesus Christ. We have given this commission to Judas and Silas, who will confirm the message by word of mouth. It is the Holy Spirit's pleasure and ours that no burden should be laid upon you beyond these, which cannot be avoided; you are to abstain from what is sacrificed to idols, from blood-meat and meat which has been strangled, and from fornication. If you keep away from such things, you will have done your part. Farewell.[43]

In different circumstances, namely among Gentile converts alone, Paul takes an approach which is different from that of the Council of Jerusalem. The decree of the latter was local and temporary in nature;[44] among the Corinthians there is no difficulty of observance among the Christians. For this reason the rights which were restricted by the Council of Jerusalem may be exercised by the Corinthians inasmuch as their exercise does not constitute a clear and present danger to the general welfare. Those same supervening principles, that the common welfare be preserved, and that scandal be avoided even in the exercise of one's rights among pagans, cause Paul to establish similar restrictions under certain circumstances. Again the text speaks for itself:

> I am free to do what I will; yes, but not everything can be done without harm. I am free to do what I will, but some things disedify. Each of you ought to study the well-being of others, not his own. When things are

[43] Acts 15:23-29.

[44] Prat, *op. cit.*, I, 117.

> sold in the open market, then you may eat them, without making any enquiries to satisfy your consciences; this world, as we know, and all that is in it belongs to the Lord. If some unbeliever invites you to his table, and you consent to go, then you need not ask questions to satisfy your consciences, you may eat whatever is put before you. But if someone says to you, This has been used in idolatrous worship, then for the sake of your informant, you must refuse to eat; it is a matter of conscience; his conscience, I mean, not yours. . . . In eating, in drinking, in all that you do, do everything as for God's glory. Give no offense to Jew, or to Greek, or to God's church. That is my own rule, to satisfy all alike, studying the general welfare more than my own, so as to win their salvation.[45]

### *Article 3. The Teaching of the Fathers*

#### A. Freedom of the Will

The *magisterium* of the Church and the teaching of Sacred Scripture are supplemented by statements from the Fathers of the Early Church concerning man's free will. The chief texts from both the Greek and Latin Fathers will demonstrate this doctrine.

##### 1. *Greek Fathers*

Among the Greek Fathers St. Justin Martyr (ca. 100/10-163/7) in his *Apologia* (150/55)[46] and in the *Dialogue with Trypho* the Jew (after 150/55)[47] expressed the freedom of man's will. In like manner St. Theophilus of Antioch (?-193?) in his letter *Ad Autoclycum* (ca. 181/2) stated this doctrine in legal

---

[45] I Corinthians 10:22, 33.

[46] *Apologia*, I, 43; Migne, *Patrologiae Cursus Completus, Series Graeca* (161 vols., Parisiis, 1857-1866), VI, col. 392 (hereafter cited as *MPG*); M. J. Rouet De Journel, *Enchiridion Patristicum loci sanctorum patrum, doctorum scriptorum ecclesiasticorum* (editio 21, Friburgi Brisgoviae: Herder, 1959), n. 123 (hereafter cited as Journel).

[47] *Dialogus cum Tryphone Iudaeo*, n. 102; *MPG*, VI, col. 713; Journel, n. 142; "Ut praeclarum (Deus) esse iudicabit, liberos ad iustitiae observationem angelos et homines creavit, ac tempore definivit quod bonum esse iudicaret eos libero uti arbitrio."

terms.[48] St. Irenaeus (ca. 140-ca. 202) in his work *Adversus haereses* taught that God created man with free will.[49] In the third century Origen (185/6-254/5) in his *Peri Archon* (ca. 230) reflected the common teaching of the Church that man enjoys free will.[50] Eusebius of Caesarea (ca. 265-340) declared that God gave freedom of choice to both men and angles at the time of their creation.[51] Toward the end of the fourth century St. John Chrysostom (344-407), in commenting on the text of Genesis, taught that the rewards promised and the punishments threatened in the next life have meaning only if one believes in free will.[52] In the fifth century St. Cyril of Alexandria (+ 444), in commenting on the text of St. John's Gospel, asserted that man's freedom of action was a gift from God.[53] The last Greek Father, St. John Damascene (675-749), at the middle of the eighth century attested to the freedom of the will in speaking of the spirituality of the soul.[54]

## 2. *Latin Fathers*

Among the Latin Fathers Tertullian (ca. 160-ca. 230) and St. Jerome (ca. 342-420) both declared that God endowed man with

---

[48] ". . . Liberum enim Deus et sui iuris hominem fecit."—*MPG,* VI, col. 1096; Journel, n. 184.

[49] ". . . liberum Deus (hominem) fecit ab initio. . . ."—*Adversus haereses,* 4, 37, 1; *MPG,* VII, 1099; Journel, n. 244.

[50] ". . . Est et illud definitum in ecclesiastica praedicatione, omnem animam rationabilem esse liberi arbitrii et voluntatis. . . ."—1, Praef., 5 referring to I Cor. 15:42; *MPG,* XI, col. 118; Journel, n. 446.

[51] *Demonstratio evangelica,* 4, 1 (shortly after 315/20)—*MPG,* XXII, col. 252; Journel, n. 667.

[52] *In Genesim homiliae,* 22, 1 (written 388)—*MPG,* LIII, col. 187; Journel, n. 1151.

[53] ". . . videndum est creatorem universae tribuisse rationalibus creaturis proprias libertatis habenas et permisisse ut irent spontaneo motu quo quisque vellet. . . ."—*In Ioannem commentarius,* 9 (13, 18) (written about or after 428); *MPG,* LXXIV, col. 129; Journel, n. 2113.

[54] "(. . . quod enim oculus in corpore, hoc mens in anima est), arbitrii libertate, volendique et agendi facultate praedita. . . ."—*De fide orthodoxa,* 2, 12 (written before 754); *MPG,* XCIV, col. 924; Journel, n. 2357.

free will at the time of creation.[55] Gennadius of Marseilles (fl. 475-500)[56] reflected the same teaching. Lastly, St. Fulgentius (468-533)[57] declared in his writings that both angels and men have free wills whereby to choose eternal salvation and the vision of God or to choose eternal damnation and suffer the loss of God.

### B. Restraint of Freedom

There would seem to be only one text of the Fathers (Tertullian) which applies to a restraint of the exercise of one's rights. The text is a statement on the practice of administration of the Sacrament of Baptism by the laity in a case of necessity.[58] Tertullian declared that the right of administering the Sacrament of Baptism belonged properly to the bishop; by delegation it belonged also to deacons and priests. Tertullian stated, however, that this same right belonged to the laity too, and could be exercised by them under certain conditions. The reason was the overriding importance of the Sacrament of Baptism for salvation.[59] Tertullian concluded his treatment of the minister of the Sacrament of Baptism with an admonition to the laity in an effort to deter the imprudent administration of this Sacrament. He referred to the text of St. Paul to the Corinthians[60] already considered, and listed the danger of death and the condition of the recipient as requirements for the licit administration of Baptism by lay people.

---

[55] Tertullianus, *Adversus Marcionem* (207/8), 2, 5: "Liberum et sui arbitrii et suae potestatis invenio hominem a Deo institutum."—*MPL,* II, 290; Journel, n. 335.

St. Hieronymus, *Adversus Iovinianum* (ca. 393), 2, 3: "Liberi arbitrii nos condidit Deus. . . ."—*MPL,* XXIII, col. 286; Journel, n. 1380.

[56] *Liber ecclesiasticorum dogmatum* (ca. 470): ". . . sed dicimus unam esse . . . animam in homine . . . haben(tem) in se libertatem arbitrii. . . ."—*MPL,* LVIII, col. 984; Journel, n. 2225.

[57] *De fide, ad Petrum—MPL,* LXV, col. 686; Journel, n. 2265.

[58] Tertullianus, *De baptismo,* n. 17; *MPL,* I, col. 1217; Journel, n. 310.

[59] ". . . etiam laicis ius (dandi et accipiendi baptismi) est . . . et baptismus . . . ab omnibus exerceri potest. . . ."—*Loc. cit.*

[60] I Cor. 10:23.

## SECTION II. THE PHILOSOPHICAL FOUNDATIONS OF FREEDOM AND ITS RESTRAINT

The unique value of the human person pertains to the essence of Thomistic philosophy.[61] This evaluation of the human person leads to certain conclusions concerning the nature of man, which affect the fields of ethics, law and politics in the practical order. Hence, it will be the object of this section to outline the underlying reasons for man's freedom and, more specifically, to establish the necessity of restraint of man's freedom by means of law as a corollary of the end of man, of the function of society, and of the relationship of man to society.

### *Article 1. Man Is Free*

Although the sources of revelation have taught us with one voice that man is by his nature a free being, Saint Thomas Aquinas, nevertheless, undertook to demonstrate man's freedom by means of human reason.[62] The proof of that argument lies outside the scope of this dissertation; it will be of service, however, to set down the broad terms of the argument, inasmuch as the conclusions drawn by the philosophers have practical bearing in the field of law.

According to Saint Thomas man is a person, that is, an individual substance of a rational nature.[63] Man exists in himself and is not dependent upon others for those actions which are proper to himself, namely, thinking and willing. Differing from other sentient beings which possess the power of locomotion, man, since he is a rational animal, enjoys complete discretion in his actions.[64] He has an intellect with which to think, and a will

---

[61] Maurice DeWulf, *Mediaeval Philosophy* (Cambridge, 1922), pp. 149, 150.

[62] St. Thomas Aquinas, *Summa Theologica* (hereafter referred to as *S.T.*), I, 83, 1—*Sancti Thomae Aquinatis Omnia Opera* (25 vols., New York: Musurgia Press, 1948), I, 323, 324 (hereafter referred to as *Omnia Opera*).

[63] St. Thomas accepted Boethius' definition of a person as found in Boethius' *Liber de Persona et de Duabus Naturis*, c. 3—*MPL*, LXIV, col. 1343. Cf. *S.T.*, I, 29, 1, in corp., and also I, 29, 3, ad 2, where a person is described as "distinctum subsistens in intellectuali natura."—*Omnia Opera*, I, 124, 125; *ibidem*, 126.

[64] *S.T.*, I, 59, 3, in corp.—*Omnia Opera*, I, 252.

with which to will or love. He can therefore apprehend with his reason what is good and true, and pursue these ideals, as apprehended by his reason, in his actions.[65] Saint Thomas puts his teaching very clearly when he says:

> . . . Man acts from judgment, because by his apprehensive power he judges that something should be avoided or sought. But because this judgment, in the case of some particular act, is not from a natural instinct, but from some act of comparison in reason, therefore he acts from free judgment and retains the power of being inclined to various things. For reason in contingent matters may follow opposite courses, as we see in dialectic syllogisms and rhetorical arguments. Now particular operations are contingent, and therefore in such matters the judgment of reason may follow opposite courses, and is not determinable to one. And inasmuch as man is rational is it necessary that man have a free will.[66]

Freedom of the will in this philosophical analysis is considered as real, physical or ontological as distinguished from psychological or moral freedom.[67] Free will in this philosophic sense means

---

[65] The will is moved not to the good as it is *in itself* but as apprehended by reason. It is in this way that St. Thomas explains mistaken judgments and evil actions; the will may perceive an "apparent good." Cf. In II Sent., dist. 39, q. 3, a. 3.—*Omnia Opera,* VI, 741-743.

[66] ". . . homo agit iudicio, quia per vim cognoscitivam iudicat aliquid esse fugiendum, vel prosequendum.—Sed quia iudicium istud non est ex naturali instinctu in particulari operabili, sed ex collatione quadam rationis: ideo agit libero iudicio, potens in diversa ferri. Ratio enim circa contingentia habet viam ad apposita, ut patet in dialectis syllogismis, et rhetoricis persuasionibus. Particularia autem operabilia sunt quaedam contingentia; et ideo circa ea iudicium rationis ad diversa se habet, et non determinatum ad unum. Et pro tanto necesse est quod homo sit liberi arbitrii ex hoc ipso quod rationalis est. . . ."—*S.T.*, I, 83, 1 in corp.—*Omnia Opera,* I, 323, 324. English translation from St. Thomas Aquinas, *Summa Theologica,* by the Fathers of the English Dominican Province (3 vols., New York: Benziger Brothers, 1947), I, 418. All English translations of St. Thomas Aquinas are taken from this translation unless otherwise noted.

[67] W. Van Ommeren, *Mental Illness Affecting Matrimonial Consent,* The Catholic University of America Canon Law Studies, n. 415 (Washington, D. C.: The Catholic University of America Press, 1961), p. 76; cf. also

freedom to act, that is, freedom from extrinsic and intrinsic restraint:[68] No external force may exert a prevailing influence upon the will and no singular good can impel the will to choose it, the ultimate good excepted, in the ordinary course of events. In a word, the will exercises an unrestricted power of self-determination.

Such freedom of action was called freedom of indifference by Scholastic philosophers.[69] From the point of view of the volitional act, this freedom is called freedom of exercise inasmuch as the will is free to act or not to act, to perform an act or to omit an act. From another point of view, namely, that of the object which is desired, and thus the freedom to choose this or that good, this freedom is called freedom of specification.[70] It is this latter kind of freedom which is subject to the external force of law in virtue of the needs of society; in like manner it is this same freedom of specification which will be legally restrained wherever this freedom is protected by juridically endowed rights.

---

*S.T.*, I-II, 10, 2—*Omnia Opera,* II, 44; *De Veritate,* q. 22, a. 5—*Omnia Opera,* IX, 319. Philosophical freedom is described as the freedom which is required for a human act. Psychological freedom is described by J. C. Ford and G. Kelly, *Contemporary Moral Theology, Volume One, Questions in Fundamental Moral Theology* (Westminster, Md.: Newman Press, 1959), p. 212. "Freely does not mean easily or without reluctance, although sometimes free choices are easily made."—*Ibidem,* p. 204.

[68] A. Rzadkiewicz, *The Philosophical Bases of Human Liberty according to St. Thomas Aquinas,* The Catholic University of America Philosophical Series, n. 105 (Washington, D. C.: The Catholic University of America Press, 1949), pp. 79, 80.

[69] H. Grenier, *Cursus Philosophiae* (3 vols., editio altera, Québec: Le Seminaire de Québec, 1944) (Vol. I), 454, n. 451; J. Maritain, *Scholasticism and Politics* (Garden City: Doubleday and Co., 1960), p. 117.

[70] There is also a moral freedom which considers the free act from the point of view of its relation to man's last end, and determines whether an act is good or evil (*De Veritate,* q. 22, a. 6—*Omnia Opera,* IX, 522-525). Moral freedom is the ability of doing what one *ought,* not what one *might,* or, in the words of one author, "Morality is the freely actualized order of reason."—H. Meyer, *The Philosophy of St. Thomas Aquinas,* trans. by Frederic Eckhoff (London: Herder, 1944), p. 369.

### *Article 2. Man Is a Social Being*

Man is by nature a social being as well as a free being.[71] He comes into this world as a member of society[72] which is the family. At birth a man is the most helpless of creatures and the obligation of his care, his education and his preparation for his life's work, rests with the family. As man advances in age and becomes more self-sustaining he naturally reaches out toward the society of his fellowmen.[73]

This largest grouping of men which is civil society serves a twofold purpose: it helps man to satisfy his material needs such as the procurement of food, drinking water, sanitation, etc., and assists him in his moral and intellectual development.[74] Civil society takes its highest and most perfect form in the state, because the state is directed to the complete fulfillment of man's essential needs in the natural order.[75] In a word, the state is the natural mode of social life for man. So long as the state performs its function of permitting man to achieve his end which is happiness, the form of government whereby the state rules its citizens is immaterial.

It is the task of the state to achieve and maintain peace and

---

[71] "(Homo) indiget ab aliis hominibus adiuvari ad consequendum proprium finem. . . ."—*Summa contra Gentiles* (hereafter cited as *S.C.G.*), Liber III, c. 117, a. 3; *ibid.*, c. 128—*Omnia Opera,* V, 255; 263, 264.

[72] A society is defined as a stable and moral union of several persons existing in order to attain the same end by means which are common to the members. Cf. A. Ottaviani, *Institutiones Iuris Publici Ecclesiastici* (2 vols.), Vol. 1, *Ecclesiae Constitutio Socialis et Potestas* (editio quarta, Romae: Typis Polyglottis Vaticanis, 1938), p. 29, n. 15.

[73] *S.T.*, II-II, 188, 8 in corp.—*Omnia Opera,* III, 636, 637.

[74] St. Thomas Aquinas, *In Libros Ethicorum,* Lib. I, lect. I; *De Regimine Principum ad Regem Cypri,* Lib. I, c. 1—*Omnia Opera,* XXI, 1-3; XVI, 225, 226.

[75] St. Thomas Aquinas, *In Libros Politicorum,* Lib. I, lect. 1—*Omnia Opera,* XXI, 362-371. Just as the state is a perfect society in the natural order inasmuch as it possesses within itself the means necessary to attain its end, so also the Church, given the fact of Revelation, as a perfect supernatural society enjoys the same kind of means in order to lead its members to its supernatural end, which is eternal salvation and the vision of God as He is in Himself. Cf. Ottaviani, *op. cit.,* I, p. 144, n. 90.

order among the citizenry.[76] The state has this task because, besides being a perfect society, it is also a necessary society, that is, it exists by the necessity of human nature and thereby possesses the authority and power of commanding and enforcing its just policies in order to serve the commonweal. In a civil society the juridic cause of society is the law and constitution under which it is founded; in the Church, however, the juridic cause of its being is its establishment by Christ, Who determined its form of government when He founded the Church. In either case, according to the nature of the institution, because it is a necessary society, the authority with which it is endowed gives it the right to bind its members in their actions by laws, injunctions, penalties, and commands, since the right of the society is greater than the rights of all of its members, taken individually and collectively, so long as its laws are just and within the domain of the society.[77]

### *Article 3. Man Lives in Society Under a Rule of Law*

The authority and power which belong to civil and ecclesiastical societies flow from their respective natures and purposes: each exists to assist man in the achievement of his end, the one in the temporal order, and the other in the spiritual order. It is only reasonable that norms would be established according to reason, whose purpose would be the right and efficient ordering of man to his end through society. This right and efficient orientation of man is the function of law. Hence it is said that Saint Thomas defines law as a reasonable command which is promulgated by the head of the community for the sake of the common welfare.[78]

Saint Thomas looks upon creation as a unity which has come into being and is continued in being by the provident power of Almighty God. Since intellect and will are identical in God Him-

---

[76] St. Thomas Aquinas, *De Regimine Principum ad Regem Cypri,* Lib. I, c. 1; *Omnia Opera,* XVI, 225, 226.

[77] ". . . boum unius hominis non est ultimus finis, sed ad commune bonum ordinatur. . . ."—*S.T.,* I-II, 90, 3, ad 3—*Omnia Opera,* II, 551, 552.

[78] ". . . lex est quaedam rationis ordinatio ad bonum commune ab eo qui curam communitatis habet promulgata. . . ."—*S.T.,* I-II, 90, 1-4;—*Omnia Opera,* II, 330-332.

self with His essence, the governance of the world will be subject to His reasonable and benevolent plan of creation. This ordering of the universe is called the eternal law.[79] In the eternal law of God are contained all other kinds of law, and upon every created being is stamped his nature and direction to his end for all eternity.

All creatures participate to some extent in the eternal law, at least in so far as from the eternal law imprinted upon them ". . . they derive their respective inclinations to their proper acts and ends."[80] The eternal law is made manifest to creatures through the activities of other creatures following the law of their natures. In the case of man the natural law takes on the character of a moral precept which is arrived at by man's reasonable analysis of the data of his experience. Saint Thomas holds that man participates in the eternal law inasmuch as he knows, and also as the inner moving principle of his activity is derived from, the eternal law; irrational creatures participate only inasmuch as their principle of action is derived from the eternal law.[81]

Saint Thomas next considers positive law in its relation to the natural law. He notes that positive law can flow from the natural law in two ways: as conclusions flow from more general principles, or as particular determinations of common sets of circumstances. In the first way, for example, from the general principle that good is to be done and evil avoided, one may conclude that murder is wrong and is to be avoided. In the second way, wherein the positive law is a particular determination for a common set of circumstances, the natural law determines the evil of the deed but leaves the punishment to be affixed by the means established by positive law. Thus unpremeditated murder will generally warrant a term of imprisonment. In this analysis Saint Thomas compares the positive legislator with an artist who applies the general

---

[79] ". . . ratio divinae sapientiae, secundum quod est directiva omnium actuum et motionum. . . ."—*S.T.*, I-II, 93, 1—*Omnia Opera*, II, 339.

[80] ". . . omnia participant aliqualiter legem aeternam, inquantum scilicit ex impressione eius habent inclinationes in proprias actus et fines."—*S.T.*, I-II, 91, 2.—*Omnia Opera*, II, 333. English translation from *Summa Theologica*, by the Fathers of the English Dominican Province, I, 997.

[81] *S.T.*, I-II, 93, 6; *Omnia Opera*, II, 341, 342.

form of art to a particular material and to particular circumstances.[82]

The laws derived from the natural law as conclusions from principles bind not only as positive laws but also as the law of nature; on the contrary, those laws which are but determinations of the natural law to conditions of time and place bind only as positive law.[83]

### *Article 4. The Function of Law: The Establishment of the Common Good*

Human law is an adjunct of positive divine law and of the law of nature. Accordingly Saint Thomas acknowledges that positive human law must serve man's benefit. Saint Thomas accepts the threefold criteria of Saint Isidore of Seville, namely, that a just law must harmonize with religion, that is, with the divine law; that a just law must provide for order (*disciplina*) inasmuch as it must agree with the natural law; and lastly, that a just law must agree with the needs of man because it is enacted for his benefit.[84] These criteria belong to law in virtue of man's end, which is his ultimate happiness and the beatific vision. In short, then, laws are made to help man lead a life in conformity with the law of God.

It should be understood, however, that although the law looks to man's perfection, it provides not for all of man's acts but for only those which are of a social nature. Saint Thomas says:

> . . . (N)evertheless human law does not prescribe concerning all the acts of every virtue: but only in regard to those that are ordainable to the common good either immediately, as when certain things are done directly for the common good, or mediately, as when a lawgiver prescribes certain things pertaining to good order, whereby the citizens are directed in the upholding of the common good of justice and peace.[85]

[82] *S.T.*, I-II, 95, 2; *Omnia Opera*, II, 348.

[83] *Loc. cit.*

[84] *S.T.*, I-II, 95, 3 *in corp.; Omnia Opera*, II, 349.

[85] ". . . Non tamen de omnibus actibus omnium virtutum lex humana praecipit, sod solum de illis quae ordinabiles sunt ad bonum commune, vel immediate, sicut cum aliqua directe propter bonum commune fiunt; vel

The community must provide that degree of peace and security which will allow individuals to follow their own ends. Saint Thomas notes[86] that, just as man is part of a family, so the family is part of the state. The state is a perfect community, and thus the private good of the individual is not the ultimate end of the state. The ultimate end of the state is the common good.[87] It is therefore possible to see how a conflict may arise between the private good of man on the one hand, and the common good of society on the other hand. Given the criteria of Saint Isidore already mentioned, it will be the function of law to preserve the common good, even, if necessary, to the exclusion of man's private good. In other words, man's basic freedom may be legally restrained when it conflicts with the common good.

### *Article 5. The Legal Restraint of Man's Freedom*

Saint Thomas Aquinas does not consider *ex professo* the legal restraint of man's freedom; nevertheless the treatment which he gives to several specific questions outlines the principles which he uses in the establishment of legally created restraints on one's freedom.

In the first place, Saint Thomas considers the binding force of human law on conscience.[88] He acknowledges that positive law may be unjust or unreasonable from several sources: laws may not further the common good and thereby be unjust because of

---

mediate, sicut cum aliqua ordinantur a legislatore pertinentia ad bonam disciplinam, per quam cives informantur, ut commune bonum iustitiae et pacis conservent."—*S.T.*, I-II, 96, 3 *in corp.; Omnia Opera,* II, 352. English translation taken from the *Summa Theologica* by the Dominican Fathers of the English Province, I, 1019.

[86] *S.T.*, I-II, 90, 3, ad 3; *Omnia Opera,* II, 332.

[87] The term "common good" has been widely misunderstood. Cf. Charles DeKoninck, "In Defense of Saint Thomas," *Laval Théologique et Philosophique,* 1 (1945), 9-109, *passim.* See also P. M. Fabregas, "Aliqua de natura boni communis," *Periodica,* XLII (1953), 246-262. Father Fabregas gives his definition of the common good on p. 260: ". . . bonum commune dicerem omne genus bonorum moralium, spiritualium, et materialium quae eis potestatem faciunt pro eorum posse vitam suasque facultates humanas ita fovendi et explicandi ut ad idoneam naturae suae progressionem tandem perveniant."

[88] *S.T.*, I-II, 96, 4; *Omnia Opera,* II, 352.

lack of due purpose; again laws may reflect an improper formulation inasmuch as they are badly constructed, even though their aim is purposeful; or laws may overreach themselves and fail because of lack of jurisdiction on the part of the legislator. In all these instances one is confronted with violations of law, or "corruptions of law" in Saint Thomas' phraseology.[89] As a general rule these laws are not endowed with any binding force; they will bind, however, notwithstanding their legislative defects, in any circumstances in which the common good of society is involved, either by reason of scandal to be avoided or by reason of some imminent civil upheaval. In these circumstances Saint Thomas states explicitly that a man should even *cede his right* according to the evangelical counsel that, "if a man compels thee to attend him on a mile's journey, go two miles with him of thy own accord; if he is ready to go to law with thee over thy coat, let him have it and thy cloak with it."[90]

Secondly, Saint Thomas in his treatment of the obedience due to superiors by their subjects states that at times the commands of superiors are contrary to the law of God, and therefore not all commands of superiors are to be obeyed.[91] As an example of such morally acceptable disobedience Saint Thomas refers to slaves and their status: their bodies may belong to their masters, but their minds are their own. On the other hand, except for those rights which belong to man naturally, such as the right to marry or to make a vow, and in the exercise of which all men are equal before God, Saint Thomas holds that masters may legitimately command their slaves under obedience, in spite of such other natural rights as the right to property and the right to spiritual development.[92]

---

[89] *Loc. cit.*

[90] ". . . Unde tales leges non obligant in foro conscientiae, nisi forte propter vitandum scandalum vel turbationem; propter quod etiam homo iure suo debet cedere, secundum illud Matth. 5:40-41."—*S.T.*, I-II, 96, 4 in corp.—*Omnia Opera*, II. 352.

[91] ". . . quandoque praecepta praelatorum sunt contra Deum. Ergo non in omnibus praelatis est obediendum."—*S.T.*, II-II, 104, 5, *Sed contra*—*Omnia Opera*, III, 379.

[92] Cf. II-II, 61, 1, 1-3; 64, 1. See also II-II, 104, I, ad 1; *Omnia Opera*, III, 228; III, 239; III, 376. In defense of Saint Thomas it must be stated

In another article of the same question[93] Saint Thomas takes up the matter of obedience to civil law. In general, civil rulers are to be obeyed because the order of justice demands it. When an unjust government imposes tyrannical commands upon the populace, however, any obligation of obedience on the part of the populace ceases, except where scandal or absolute chaos will result from the disobedience.[94] In that exceptional case the common good demands that such a despotic government be obeyed.

Saint Thomas repeats this doctrine again when he touches upon the sinfulness of sedition. The general principle is that a tyrannical government is not just, since it is directed not to the common good but to the private good of the tyrant.[95] In this case revolution is not sedition and therefore not sinful. There is the exceptional case, however, in which the subject multitude would suffer greater harm from the consequent revolution than from the continuance of the tyrannical regime. In this case the malice of the sin of sedition would be present and one would have to suffer the tyrant.

In his commentary on the fifth book of Aristotle's Nichomachean Ethics, Saint Thomas speaks of the nature of the commonwealth and the kind of rights which the citizenry possesses:

> Laws are passed to ensure the smooth running of the commonwealth. Unrestricted rights are not allowed in any civil constitution. Even in a democratic state, where the whole people exercise power, rights are not absolute but relative, though from the equal liberty of all subjects under the law the state may be described as predominantly egalitarian. The statutes passed by a democracy must be just, not because they reach pure and perfect justice, but because they fit the purpose of the regime.[96]

that he was writing in the thirteenth century in a different political, social, educational, and economic milieu; moreover, it is possible that Saint Thomas discussed this point as a theoretical proposition.

[93] *S.T.*, II-II, 104, 6, ad 3; *Omnia Opera,* III, 381.

[94] ". . . si non habent iustum principatum, sed usurpatum, vel si iniusta praecipiant, non tenentur eis subditi obedire; nisi forte per accidens, propter vitandum scandalum vel periculum."—*Loc. cit.*

[95] *S.T.*, II-II, 42, 2, ad 3; *Omnia Opera,* III, 161.

[96] ". . . Omnis lex datur in ordine ad aliquam politiam: non autem in omni politia est simpliciter iustum, sed in quibusdam est iustum solum secundum

In fine, one may conclude from these several texts of Saint Thomas Aquinas that the nature of man and the function of law and society in the pursuit of the common good demand that man's individual freedom be restrained where it interferes with the attainment of the common good. This restriction of rights is true of civil society which is geared to the attainment of man's natural end; *a fortiori* this restrictive power will belong to the Church, which has been commissioned by Christ Himself to lead men to salvation and the vision of the Triune God.

It remains now to consider the nature of the persons affected by this kind of restriction as well as the nature of the rights which are subject to these restrictions. Both of these topics will be treated in the next chapter.

---

quid . . . nam in politia democratica, in qua populus totus vult dominari, attenditur iustum secundum quid, sed non simpliciter; ut scilicet quia omnes cives sunt aequales secundum quid, scilicet secundum libertatem, ideo habeantur aequales simpliciter. Unde ea quae secundum legem democraticam statuuntur non sunt simpliciter iusta, sed aliqualiter. Dicit autem illa esse legalia, quae sunt statuta et determinata per legem positivam, quae competit legislatoribus. Et unumquodque eorum sic determinatorum dicitur aliqualiter iustum."—St. Thomas Aquinas, *In decem libros Ethicorum Aristotelis ad Nichomachum expositio,* cura et studio Raymundi M. Spiazzi, O.P. (Taurini-Romae: Marietti, 1949), pp. 246, 247. English translation taken from *Saint Thomas Aquinas: Philosophical Texts* (edited by Thomas Gilbey, New York: Oxford University Press, 1951), Community and Society, The Political Community, n. 1099, p. 386.

# CHAPTER VI

## THE SUBJECT AND OBJECT OF THE LEGAL RESTRAINT OF RIGHTS

The previous chapter laid the theological and philosophical foundations for the restraint of freedom. It will be recalled that the common good of natural society and the salvation of man as a member of a supernatural society have provided the motives whereby man's innate freedom has been subjected to legal restrictions. This chapter will consider the individual person in his juridic capacity and those rights which accrue to him by law and which may be restrained.

### SECTION I. THE SUBJECT OF LEGAL RESTRAINT

The legal restraint of a person in Canon Law is founded on his juridic capacity in the Church, which is a consequence of a person's membership in a legally constituted society. The Church has been defined as a society,[1] that is, a union of men who are bound together both by the profession of the same faith and the sharing of the same sacraments under the governance of legitimately appointed pastors, and especially the Holy Father. Pope Pius XII (1939-1958) in his encyclical *Mystici Corporis* issued on June 29, 1943, referred to the Church in its social and juridic nature. He reproved any conception of the Church as a moral, invisible union of men; the Pontiff, moreover, positively affirmed the connection between the order of grace and conscience, on the one hand, and the juridic external order, on the other hand, as real

[1] "Coetus hominum viatorum, eiusdem fidei Christianae professione, et eorundem sacramentorum communione adunatus, sub regimine legitimorum pastorum, ac praecipue Romani Pontificis."—R. Bellarminus, *Disputationes de controversiis,* 4 vols., Liber III, *De ecclesia* (Venetiis, 1599), c. II—cited by Ottaviani, *op. cit.*, I, n. 88. Ottaviani added the word "viatorum" to Cardinal Bellarmine's definition of the Church as more descriptive of the Church's function.

and actual in the Roman Catholic Church.[2] The Holy Father went further in declaring that the Church is not adequately described as a moral union of men after the manner of a moral person or, contrarily, an absolutely physical union of men, that is, a union of those only who are professing Catholics, but a visible, external, and unique society which is called mystical inasmuch as the Church has Christ as the Principle of unity.[3] The Church is therefore a supernatural society because Christ is the Founder and the Head. It is Christ Himself Who has established the Church and has determined the qualifications for membership in the Church.

### *Article 1. Juridical Personality in the Church*

It will be recalled that personality in its philosophical sense is dependent upon the fact of humanity, that is, the existence in the body of a rational soul. It follows, then, that any man inasmuch as he is a man, from the moment of his conception, during his prenatal existence, and all during his life is a person and thereby endowed with rights flowing from the divine law, both positive

---

[2] The text speaks of an alleged distinction between the Church "utpote societatem quamdam caritate alitam ac formatam" and a Church "quam iuridicam vocant." The Holy Father answers: ". . . non enim intelligunt divinum Redemptorem eadem ipsa de causa conditum a se hominum coetum, perfectam voluisse genere suo societatem constitutam, ac iuridicis omnibus socialibusque elementis instructam, ut nempe salutiferum Redemptionis opus hisce in terris perennaret; et ad eundem finem assequendum coelestibus eam voluisse donis ac muneribus a Paraclito Spiritu ditatam."—*AAS,* XXXV (1943), 224.

[3] "In hoc enim (corpore), quod morale vocant, nihil aliud est unitatis principium, nisi finis communis, communisque omnium in eundem finem per socialem, auctoritatem conspiratio; dum in mystico, de quo agimus, Corpore conspirationi huic internum aliud adiungitur principium, quod tam in universa compage, quam in singulis eius partibus reapse existens virtuteque pollens, talis est excellentiae, ut ratione sui omnia unitatis vincula, quibus vel physicum vel morale corpus copuletur, in immensum prorsus evincat. Hoc est . . . aliquid non naturalis, sed superni ordinis, immo in semetipso infinitum omnino atque increatum: Divinus nempe Spiritus, qui, ut sit Angelicus (*De Veritate,* q. 29, a. 4, corp) 'unus et idem numero, totam Ecclesiam replet et unit.'"—*AAS,* 35 (1943), 222.

and natural.[4] It is this humanity of man which makes him eligible for ecclesiastical personality.[5]

Just as it is a fact that juridic personality arises from law, whether divine (positive or natural) or human (civil or ecclesiastical), so in each case the nature of the personality is dependent upon its legal origin.[6] In the Church the source of juridic personality is the fact of baptism with water and that alone.[7] The necessity of baptism as a requirement for incorporation into the Church has incessantly been taught by the ordinary *magisterium* of the Church. This same teaching has also been reflected in theological writings.[8] The theological implications of the necessity of baptism for incorporation into the Church and the juridic consequences flowing therefrom were recapitulated by the late Pope Pius XII in his encyclical *Mystici Corporis* in which

---

[4] C. Piontek, "De Acephalis in Iure Canonico," *Ius Pontificium,* XIV (1934), 194-215; 284-294; XV (1935), 56-63; 202-208; XVII (1937), 64-82. The present citation is to be found in XIV (1934), 214.

[5] "Subiectum capax baptismi est omnis et solus homo viator, nondum baptizatus."—Canon 745, § 1.

[6] G. Michiels, *Normae Generales Iuris Canonici, Commentarius Libri I Codicis Iuris Canonici* (2 vols., ed. altera, Parisiis-Tornaci-Romae: Desclée et Socii, 1949), I, 4, 5; *Principia Generalia de Personis in Ecclesia, Commentarius Libri II Codicis Iuris Canonici, Canones Praeliminares* (2. ed. penitus retractata et notabiliter aucta, Parisiis-Tornaci-Romae: Desclée et Socii, 1955), p. 10; W. Onclin, "Considerationes de iurium subiectivorum in Ecclesia fundamento ac natura," *Ephemerides Iuris Canonici,* VIII (1952), 9-11.

[7] During the pontificate of S. Leo IV (847-855) the Council of Valence (855) taught: ". . . firmissime tenendum credimus, quod omnis multitudo fidelium *ex aqua et Spiritu Sancto* regenerata, ac per hoc veraciter Ecclesiae incorporata. . . ."—Denz., n. 324; Pope Eugene IV (1431-1447) in the Bull *Exultate Deo* of Nov. 22, 1439, required in the profession of faith of the Armenians: "Primum omnium sacramentorum locum tenet sanctum baptisma . . . per ipsum enim membra Christi ac de corpore efficimur Ecclesiae."—Denz., n. 696; cf. also Denz., n. 895. In Sacred Scripture, cf. John 3:5; Mt. 28:19; I Cor. 12:27.

[8] St. Thomas Aquinas taught that baptism is the principle of spiritual life and the door to the other Sacraments (*S.T.,* III, 73, 3, in corp.—*Omnia Opera,* IV, 334), and the Sacrament whereby man is numbered among the congregation of the faithful (*S.T.,* III, 70, 1, in corp.—*Omnia Opera,* IV, 319).

the Pontiff stated that the requirements for membership in the juridic, visible society of the Church were: the fact of baptism with water, the profession of the true faith, the maintenance of the bond of communion, and the lack of excommunication by legitimate authority.[9] These requirements distinguish between Catholics, heretics, schismatics, apostates, and excommunicates and their relation to the law of the Church.

The Code of Canon Law incorporated these requirements in canon 87[10] as expressed in the Pauline teaching that each Christian was called "with the same Lord, the same faith, the same baptism."[11] Yet it is an obvious fact that not all the baptized are members of the external visible society which is the Church. What then is the juridic capacity of the validly baptized non-Catholics? The legal principle whereby a viable legal status is attributed to validly baptized non-Catholics is found in the latter half of canon 87,[12] and will be considered in the next article. It suffices for the moment to point out the fact that personality in the Church, while always present by virtue of the reception of the Sacrament of Baptism, is subject to modifications by the law.[13] Two of these modifications of personality, namely age and the use of reason, are intrinsic to the person and merit separate treatment.

### A. Age

The Code of Canon Law has laid down categories of persons according to age in canon 88. A person in his majority is defined as one who has completed his twenty-first year of age.[14] That age

[9] "In Ecclesiae membris reapse ii soli annumerandi sunt, qui regenerationis lavacrum receperunt veramque fidem profitentur, neque a corporis compage semetipsos misere separarunt, vel ob gravissima admissa a legitima auctoritate seiuncti sunt."—*AAS*, XXXV (1943), 202.

[10] "Baptismate homo constituitur in Ecclesia Christi persona cum omnibus christianorum iuribus et officiis nisi, ad iura quod attinet, obstet obex, ecclesiasticae communionis vinculum impediens, vel lata ab Ecclesia censura."

[11] Ephesians 4:5.

[12] Cf. *supra*, footnote 10.

[13] Ph. Maroto, *Institutiones Iuris Canonici ad Normam Novi Codicis* (2 vols., Vol. I, 3. ed., Matriti, 1921), I, nn. 390, 392.

[14] "Persona quae vicesimum primum aetatis annum explevit, maior est; infra hanc aetatem, minor."—Canon 88, § 1.

is reached upon one's natural birthday anniversary plus one day since Canon Law does not include parts of days, but includes only whole days in its computing of time.[15] Ordinarily a person who has achieved his majority has attained full physical, intellectual and moral maturity and enjoys the full exercise of his rights and is a responsible person before the law. Conversely, anyone who has not reached the canonical age of twenty-one is deemed by the law to be a minor.

The law distinguishes several kinds of minors. Among minors there are some who have reached the age of puberty (*puberes*) and others who have not yet reached that age (*impuberes*). The law further distinguishes *infantes* and *parvuli* or *infantia egressi* among the *impuberes*.[16]

### 1. *Puberty*

Canon 88, § 2, states that the age of puberty for boys is fourteen years of age completed, and for girls twelve years of age completed.[17] The age of puberty is generally taken to mean the age at which a person becomes physically able to procreate.[18] It must be understood, however, that this delimitation of age simply serves as a legal convenience for establishing juridical relationships, and is not a determination on the part of the law of an existent physical capability for marriage. The law itself takes cognizance of this point in canon 1067, § 1,[19] which gives the age of sixteen years completed for boys and fourteen years completed for girls as the absolute minimal age at which marriage may be validly contracted.

It appears that the statement of canon 88, § 2, sets up a

---

[15] "Si terminus *a quo* non coincidat cum initio diei . . . primus dies ne computetur et tempus finiatur expleto ultimo die eiusdem numeri."—Canon 34, § 3, 3°.

[16] Canon 88, §§ 2 and 3.

[17] "Minor, si masculus, censetur pubes a decimoquarto, si femina, a duodecimo anno completo."—Canon 88, § 2.

[18] G. Michiels, *Principia Generalia de Personis in Ecclesia*, pp. 38, 39.

[19] "Vir ante decimum sextum aetatis annum completum, mulier ante decimum quartum item completum, matrimonium validum inire non possunt."

presumption of law, that is, a fiction of law which is established by the lawgiver as a norm of action and which, if verified in its factual basis, is taken as a legal means of proof.[20] Authors have differed on the question whether this presumption as mentioned in canon 88, § 2, is a *praesumptio iuris simpliciter* or a *praesumptio iuris et de iure.* The former presumption admits proof either against the presumption itself or against its factual basis; the latter presumption, however, admits proof only against its factual basis.[21] In other words, one is faced with two situations: one may look upon the presumption as valid until it is contradicted by evidence, or one may look upon the presumption as always valid unless there be other provision even though its factual basis may occasionally be found wanting. In the case of canon 88, § 2, there is question of a *praesumptio iuris simpliciter* if it is considered that a boy who is able to procreate before the completion of his fourteenth year is of the legal age of puberty, or, conversely, that a boy who is beyond the canonical age of fourteen but is not yet able to procreate is not of the legal age of puberty. This is the opinion of Beste,[22] O'Donnell[23] and Conte a Coronata.[24] There is question of a *praesumptio iuris et de iure* if canon 88, § 2, is construed as comprehending all those and only those who have arrived at the canonical age of puberty, in abstraction altogether from the physical ability to procreate. This is the opinion of Michiels,[25] and Piontek.[26]

---

[20] "Praesumptio est rei incertae probabilis coniectura."—Canon 1825, § 1. The juridical effect of presumptions is given in canon 1827: "Qui habet pro se iuris praesumptionem, liberatur ab onere probandi, quod recidit in partem adversam. . . ."

[21] Canon 1826.

[22] U. Beste, *Introductio in Codicem* (4. ed., Neapoli: M. D'Auria, Pontificius Editor, 1956), pp. 135, 136.

[23] C. O'Donnell, *The Marriage of Minors,* The Catholic University of America, Canon Law Series, n. 221 (Washington, D. C.: The Catholic University of America Press, 1945), p. 76.

[24] M. Conte a Coronata, *Institutiones Iuris Canonici* (4 vols., Vols. I-III, 4. ed., Vol. IV, 3. ed., Taurini: Marietti, 1950-1956), I, n. 120.

[25] *Principia Generalia de Personis,* p. 40.

[26] "Art. cit.," *Ius Pontificium,* XVII (1937), 65.

### 2. *Minors Below the Age of Puberty*

Canon 88, § 3, separates children below the age of puberty into two groups: *infantes* and *parvuli* or *infantia egressi.*[27] The *infantes* are those who have not completed their seventh year and are not held in any way responsible before the law (*non sui compotes*). Once the canonical age of seven has been reached these *infantia egressi* are presumed by the law to have the use of reason.[28]

## B. Use of Reason

Canon 88, § 3, identifies those who are habitually destitute of the use of their reason with *infantes* at law.[29] No mention is made of those who are *actually,* although not habitually, deprived of the use of their reason. Their status at law must be culled from a juxtaposition of two other canons with canon 88, § 3.

One of the requirements of Canon Law which binds a person to the observance of merely ecclesiastical law is the *actual* enjoyment of the use of reason.[30] Although the term is not employed in canon 12, one may speak of the actual use of reason as implicit in the word *gaudent,* which is used in the canon. This concept is found expressly stated in canon 2201, §§ 1 and 3,[31] which exempts persons actually bereft of reason of any delictual responsibility. Even if a delict is committed by them in such a state, they are not

---

[27] "Impubes, ante plenum septennium, dicitur infans seu puer vel parvulus et censetur non sui compos; expleto autem septennio, usum rationis habere praesumitur. . . ."—Canon 88, § 3.

[28] Authors are agreed that this paragraph of canon 88 refers to a presumption *iuris simpliciter.* Cf. Michiels, *Principia Generalis de Personis in Ecclesia,* p. 47; Beste, *op. cit.,* p. 136; O'Donnell, *op. cit.,* p. 77; J. McCloskey, *The Subject of Ecclesiastical Law according to Canon 12,* The Catholic University of America, Canon Law Studies, n. 165 (Washington, D. C.: The Catholic University of America Press, 1943), pp. 199-201.

[29] "Infanti assimilantur quotquot usu rationis sunt habitu destituti." Canon 88, § 3.

[30] "Legibus mere ecclesiasticis non tenentur . . . baptizati qui sufficienti rationis usu non gaudent. . . ."—Canon 12.

[31] "Delicti sunt incapaces qui *actu* carent usu rationis . . . violata autem lege in ebrietate involuntaria, imputabilitas exsulat omnino, si ebrietas usum rationis adimat ex toto. . . ."

to be held as responsible. The canon speaks of drunkenness, but applies the same norm to other kinds of mental disturbances.[82]

Michiels summarizes the law of the Code with respect to the use of reason.[83] The lawgiver distinguishes two kinds of mentally disturbed persons at law: (1) Those who are completely deprived of the use of their reason; (2) Those who are not completely deprived of the use of their reason. Within the first group are those who habitually or actually, that is, momentarily, are bereft of their reason. Within the second group are those who enjoy the use of their reason in a diminished state, either because of a mental disturbance or because of some weakness of mind.

The fact of habitual or actual loss of reason is determinable at law by means of a judicial decision. The judge should call in experts to determine the psychological status of the subject's mind.[84] The Code states that the judge should arrive at moral certitude from the acts and evidence of the case,[85] even with regard to the testimony of experts, and make his own decision, taking into consideration not only the conclusions of the experts but also the arguments upon which these conclusions are based.[86] The intention of the law in assessing the responsibility of a person whose sanity is in dispute is not so much an investigation of the mental illness from which the person suffers as it is an assessment of the psychological effects upon the subject's use of reason.[87] Many mental disturbances may have similar if not identical effects

---

[82] "Idem dicatur de aliis similibus mentis perturbationibus."—Canon 2201, § 3.

[83] *Principia Generalia de Personis in Ecclesia,* p. 72.

[84] Canon 1792.

[85] Canon 1869, §§ 1 and 2.

[86] Canon 1804, § 1.

[87] "Nella scienza giuridica e teologica . . . l'infermità mentale viene presa in considerazione non già in se stessa, sibbene appunto e soltanto in quelle che sono le sue ripercussioni e le sue conseguenze sulla responsabilità e l'imputabilità dell' infermo, onde ciò che interessa al teologo e al giurista non è già di ricercare e di stabilire quale sia, nella quasi infinita varietà di alienazioni mentali, la *species,* in cui debba classificarsi quella in esame nel caso concreto in relazione alla natura, alle note caratteristiche ed alle varie manifestazioni che valgono ad individuarla ed a differenziarla dalle altre, quanto d'indagare ed accertare quali siano i suoi effetti sulla capacità d'intendere e di volere dell'individuo che ne è effeto in rapporto all'atto che deve compiere o che ha già compiuto: anche invero le specie piu lontane e

in the subject, and since one must proceed from effect to cause in any analysis, there is danger in a misdirected analysis. Once the effect of the insanity upon responsibility has been attained, a person may be classed as either actually or habitually insane for legal purposes.

### *Article 2. Moral Personality in the Church*

Besides physical persons in the Church there are also moral persons. The Code of Canon Law gives no formal definition of a moral person, but the general notion of a moral person may be deduced from a comparison of canons 87, 99 and 101, § 1. According to the usual Aristotelian four causes, a moral person is any and every juridic entity, distinct from a physical person, existing in the Church (material cause, canon 99) which has been established by public authority (efficient cause, canon 99) as a subject of rights and obligations (formal cause, canons 87 and 99) for a religious or charitable purpose (final cause, canon 100, § 1).[38] Moral persons are of two kinds in Canon Law: collegiate and non-collegiate moral persons.[39]

#### A. Collegiate Moral Persons

A collegiate moral person is one which is established from a group of several physical persons, the minimum requisite number being three.[40] The collegiate moral person is a legal entity which is distinct from the members which compose it: as a result, the rights of the collegiate moral person are not those of the members, nor likewise are the obligations of the one the obligations of the other.[41]

---

diverse di *amentia* hanno per lui lo stesso identico valore, se identici siano i loro effetti nei riguardi della *discretio iudicii* dei singoli individui che ne sono affetti."—P. D'Avack, *Cause di nullità e di divorzio* (2 vols., 2. ed., Firenze: Casa Editrice del Dott. Carlo Cya, 1952), I, 185.

[38] A. Lobo, "Tiene la Acción Catolica personalidad moral eclesiastica?" *Revista Española de Derecho Canonico,* VII (1952), 291.

[39] Canon 99.

[40] Canon 100, § 2.

[41] F. Wernz-P. Vidal, *Ius Canonicum ad Normam Codicis Exactum* (7 vols. in 8, Romae: Apud Aedes Universitatis Gregorianae), Vol. II (3. ed., 1943), 35 (hereafter cited as Wernz-Vidal).

### B. Non-collegiate Moral Persons

A non-collegiate moral person consists not of physical persons but of property and resources which are separated from the ownership of other persons and dedicated to a religious or charitable purpose.[42] Canon 99 lists churches, seminaries and benefices as examples of non-collegiate moral persons.

The juridic capacity of moral persons in the Church is comparable to that of physical persons. Moral persons can acquire and possess all rights coming to physical persons except those which by the natural law or positive prescription belong only to physical persons.[43] Moral persons are granted by the law special protection in the exercise of their rights inasmuch as they are considered as minors in their actions.[44]

## SECTION II. THE OBJECT OF LEGAL RESTRAINT

The first section of this chapter connoted an attempt to outline the nature of personality in Canon Law in so far as personality is subject to legal restraint. In a word, the aim was to answer the question: whose rights are subject to restriction by the law. This second section will attempt a summary of the juridical notion of right in law, describe the kinds of rights with which Canon Law deals, and finally compare the enjoyment of rights with the intrinsic qualities of personality already described.

### *Article 1. The Nature of Right*

The concept of right in law is a consequence of the nature of man and his relation to society. According to the Christian conception of man it may be said that man possesses an absolute value in himself; it may also be said that he is not the mere creature of the state, but is oriented toward a goal which is properly his own.

---

[42] T. L. Bouscaren-A. C. Ellis, *Canon Law, A Text and Commentary* (3. rev. ed., Milwaukee: Bruce Publishing Company, 1957), p. 86 (hereafter cited as Bouscaren-Ellis).

[43] Michiels, *Principia Generalia de Personis in Ecclesias,* p. 455.

[44] Canon 100, § 3: Personae morales sive collegiales sive non collegiales minoribus aequiparantur.

It is the function of society and of the law, therefore, to acknowledge these facts and to afford legal implementation to them. The law achieves this implementation and protection of man through rights whereby man is defended from the intrusions of all other men or of society itself in his attainment of his proper end. Hence it follows that a right is a relationship between persons (physical and moral) concerning actions, omissions, permissions and prohibitions in concrete circumstances. A right is therefore definable as a relation existing between one person and the action or omission of another, according to which the former may demand this action or omission as due to him on the strength of the equality of men, in virtue of the common good, and the goal of happiness toward which all men strive.[45]

It is a fact of experience that rights do not exist in a vacuum. Rights exist or come into being in persons, that is, in subjects of rights. From the point of view of the subject who possesses a right, a right may be defined as a moral and inviolable faculty of ordering things to one's proper end, i.e., of having, doing or choosing certain things.[46]

### *Article 2. Kinds of Rights*

It will be recalled that man is subject to different kinds of law. All men are subject, first of all, to the divine law. It is in this sense that the Church recognizes man's natural personality and the legal effects of acts entered into between the baptized and unbaptized.[47] The Church, moreover, has been entrusted by Christ with the task of authentically interpreting and teaching the law of God and the rights and obligations contained therein. Even

---

[45] L. Bender, *Philosophia Iuris* (2. ed., Romae: Officium Libri Catholici, 1955), p. 67; R. Begin, *Natural Law and Positive Law,* The Catholic University of America, Canon Law Series, No. 393 (Washington, D. C.: The Catholic University of America Press, 1959), pp. 14, 15.

[46] "[Ius subiectivum] . . . est facultas moralis inviolabilis ordinandi quaedam ad proprium finem, seu quaedam habendi, faciendi vel exigendi."—F. Saurez, *Tractatus de legibus* (Antwerpiae, 1631), Lib. I, cap. 2, n. 4; A. Van Hove, *Prolegomena,* p. 6, n. 2.

[47] Michiels, *Principia Generalia de Personis in Ecclesia,* p. 15; Onclin, "art. cit.," p. 13.

though the unbaptized are not recognized as juridic persons in the Church, nevertheless this interpretation binds the unbaptized just as much as the baptized because of the nature of the law. While it is true to say that some rights and obligations of the divine law are contained in the Code of Canon Law, yet, to put the matter in its proper perspective, it must also be pointed out that Canon Law as a general rule concerns itself with the baptized and with those rights which accrue to the baptized from ecclesiastical law.

Some authors, notably Ciprotti[48] and Gismondi,[49] have held that the non-baptized have a limited juridic personality in the Church and possess some rights in Canon Law by virtue of the natural law. It is argued that the non-baptized are prevented from possessing rights publicly in the Church, but are not prevented from acquiring some rights in the Church. They are not members of the Church but, analogously with civil law, they possess private rights as *peregrini* or as citizens of one state who reside in another state and possess rights which are recognized outside their proper jurisdiction.

It is argued against this opinion that the non-baptized have a natural personality which the Church recognizes in the legal effects of juridical relations between the baptized and the non-baptized, as for example in the ability of the non-baptized to contract valid marriages with the baptized. It is further argued, by Onclin in particular,[50] that one must distinguish between the Church teaching and the Church governing. It is indeed true that authentic declarations of the *magisterium* of the Church concerning divine law bind the unbaptized as much as the baptized; such authentic declarations represent the Church teaching. These same authentic declarations may receive canonical sanction by the Church governing which will be applied to the membership of the Church. Thus it may happen that these authentic declarations will impose new

---

[48] "Personalità e Battesimo nel diritto della Chiesa," *Il Diritto Ecclesiastico,* LIII (1942), 273-276.

[49] "Gli acatolici nel diritto della Chiesa," *Ephemerides Iuris Canonici,* II (1946), 224-249; III (1947), 20-55; IV (1948), 55-68. The citation is found in II (1946), 237.

[50] W. Onclin, "art. cit.," p. 14.

obligations *coram Ecclesia* upon the baptized exclusively. Moreover, the distinction between public and private rights among the unbaptized in regard to the Church is deniable as a gratuitous assertion. Canon 87 states that baptism constitutes a man as a person in the Church and makes no distinction between private and public rights.

Another argument against the opinion of Ciprotti and Gismondi is that the Code of Canon Law does not incorporate as a general rule the precepts of the positive or natural divine law, but is a codification in general of ecclesiastical law.[51] Onclin adds a historical argument,[52] namely, that the principles of the natural law are not incorporated into the Code of Canon Law by virtue of canon 6, 6°,[53] which abrogated all positive ecclesiastical law unless that law is contained in the Code, in liturgical books, or unless that law is of the positive or natural divine law. The writer is of the opinion that a careful reading of canon 6, 6°, will lead one to agree with Onclin that not all of the natural law is contained in the Code of Canon Law. On that basis it is hard to justify the opinion of Ciprotti and Gismondi.

Another controversy arises concerning the restriction of the free exercise of rights contained in the Code of Canon Law and the strict interpretation given to restricted rights. Three opinions are held on this point. They will be investigated separately.

Vermeersch[54] held that all ecclesiastical laws, except those which directly or positively granted a favor or conferred a benefice, of whatever kind and for whatever purpose which restricted the

---

[51] ". . . principia iuris naturalis remanent regulae in ordine morali, non in ordine iuridico, per auctoritatem publicam non coercibiles, nisi in quantum per legem positivam ecclesiasticam proponuntur et applicantur."—Van Hove, *Prolegomena,* p. 60, n. 54.

[52] Onclin, "art. cit.," p. 15.

[53] "Si qua et ceteris disciplinaribus legibus, quae usque adhuc viguerunt, nec explicite nec implicite in Codice contineatur, ea vim omnem amisisse dicenda est, nisi in probatis liturgicis libris reperiatur, aut lex sit iuris divini sive positivi sive naturalis." Canon 6, 5° and 6° refer only to universal penal and disciplinary laws: cf. A. Cicognani, *Canon Law,* p. 507.

[54] A. Vermeersch, *Theologia Moralis* (4 vols., 4. ed., Romae-Brugis, 1926), I, n. 197; *Epitome Iuris Canonici* (3 vols., 3. ed. Mechliniae-Romae, 1927), I, n. 98.

native liberty of Christians and imposed a burden that would not otherwise be present except for the law, were to be strictly interpreted. Vermeersch held, moreover, that a person enjoys inviolable rights in his private life, and that among the most cherished of these is his personal freedom.[55]

Another author, Falco,[56] is of the opinion that laws which restrain the free exercise of rights are nothing else but exceptions to more general laws. Aside from these exceptional laws which are to be strictly interpreted by virtue of Canon 19,[57] all laws are to be broadly interpreted. The reason is that the Church was instituted by Christ for the supernatural purpose of man's salvation. The Church was charged by Christ with this responsibility and in the fulfillment of this duty has established laws to achieve that purpose. Thus it happens that man's natural freedom is necessarily restricted within limits by the divine law and by positive ecclesiastical law. The result is that the Church does not restrict rights but rather enacts laws which are constitutive or determinative of rights themselves.

The third opinion is the more common one.[58] This opinion distinguishes between two kinds of freedom. The first kind of freedom is called negative or generic, since it arises from the absence of any prohibitive or prescriptive enactment of law. The second kind of freedom is called positive and specific, since it arises from an actual grant or concession of either divine or ecclesiastical law. The law of the Code of Canon Law, according to this opinion, refers to the second kind of freedom which is positively enacted. Hence it follows that those laws alone which restrain the exercise

---

[55] Vermeersch speaks of *iura* ". . . quae a persona habentur, ita ut saltem aliis privatis sint per se inviolabilia. Inter iura ipsa libertas computanda est hoc vel illud ex propria electione faciendi, cum divinitus concessa sit libertas agendi intra limites praeceptorum." *Epitome Iuris Canonici, Loc. cit.*

[56] *Introduzione allo studio del Codex Iuris Canonici* (Torino, 1925), pp. 102, 103.

[57] "Leges quae poenam statuunt, aut liberum iurium exercitium coarctant, aut exceptionem a lege continent, strictae subsunt interpretationi."

[58] Michiels, *Normae Generales,* I, 574; Van Hove, *De legibus ecclesiasticis,* nn. 302-305; A. Vermeersch-J. Creusen, *Epitome Iuris Canonici* (3 vols., 7. ed., Mechliniae-Romae: Dessain, 1949-1956), I, 125, n. 126; Werz-Vidal, II, p. 232, n. 178.

of rights directly and positively granted by the law, divine or human, are subject to strict interpretation.

The opinion of Vermeersch fails because of the narrow definition of right which does not take account of the legitimate obligations of the person to society and public authority to which man's freedom is subject by the divine law.[59] The first opinion is also defective because there are many matters contained in the Code of Canon Law which restrict freedom but do not injure any right; so, for example, there are laws which govern access to the hierarchy of order or jurisdiction and the exercise of offices in the Church. The opinion of Falco neglects to consider the wording of canon 19, which expressly distinguishes between laws which restrain the free exercise of rights and laws which contain exceptions to the general law. Furthermore, the Code of Canon Law has within it laws which restrain the free exercise of rights.[60] The third opinion enjoys the advantage of limiting the restriction of man's freedom to those instances in which the law has clothed that freedom with positive rights. Such restrictions come within the purview of the juridical order, moreover, and as a result man's freedom is protected at law, for it is the purpose of law to establish a rule of reason and justice within the community. Within the limitations of frail human nature, justice is attainable through law and through legal institutions. It has never been known in the history of mankind that justice has been maintained outside of a rule of law.

## *Article 3. The Effects of Juridical Personality in the Church*

### A. Persons Enjoying Full Membership in the Church

#### 1. *Majors*

Just as canon 88 separates persons in the Church according to age and the use of reason, so canon 89 lists the legal effects of this separation. The general principle of canon 89 is that a person who has attained the canonical age of majority has the full and free exercise of his rights. No mention is made in canon 89 of

[59] Van Hove, *De legibus ecclesiasticis,* n. 303.

[60] Canons 595, § 3; 1039, § 1; 1672 and ff.

the requirement of the law of a more advanced age for the purpose of acquiring certain rights.[61]

The prescription of canon 88, § 3, identifies those who are habitually destitute of the use of their reason with infants in the eyes of the law. The legal effects of this canon are far-reaching. In the first place, a person must have the use of his reason according to canon 12 in order to be bound by ecclesiastical law. If a man comes to the age of his majority without the use of his reason or loses the use of his reason after reaching majority, the law itself protects him by limiting him in the exercise of his rights.

The concept of juridical personality given in canon 87 and the status of persons in their majority in the general law of the Church as contained in canon 89 are given further extension with regard to procedural capacity in the Code of Canon Law in canon 1646. Therein it is stated that anyone who is not forbidden by law may introduce an action before an ecclesiastical tribunal, and that one who is legitimately called into court by an action must answer the charge. Canon 1647 adds that at times, when either the law or the judge requires it, both parties must be physically present in court, even though the parties are represented by attorneys in order that the parties' rights may be adequately protected.

The law allows in three instances the restriction of the procedural rights of persons in their majority. In the first place, the judge is empowered by law to declare a person a spendthrift (*bonis interdictus*) and can forbid such a person to act or answer a charge personally, and allow action in court only through his guardian (*curator*).[62] The guardian in question may be one appointed by the civil law, if the guardian is approved by the proper ordinary of the party, or the ordinary has the option of appointing a suitable person to fulfill this duty, if the ordinary deems it prudent. A person who is interdicted can only act by himself at law to answer criminal charges of personal delicts. Secondly, canon 1650 applies these same norms and exceptions to the feeble-minded (*ii qui minus firmae mentis sunt*). One author would include the blind, the deaf and the dumb in this category, if any of these can-

---

[61] Cf. canons 331, § 1, 2°; 434, § 1; 1573, § 4.

[62] Canon 1650.

not provide for themselves.[63] In the third place, canon 1648, § 1, renders those who are habitually destitute of the use of their reason incapable of acting or of answering charges before the law in their person, but allows action only through their guardians.

2. *Minors*

Canon 89 subjects minors to the power of their parents or guardians (*tutores*) in the exercise of their rights, except in those instances in which the law exempts them from parental subjection. Again, this is a general statement of principle, and one must go to particular examples. The term *parents* includes, first of all, the father according to canon 1648, § 3; then, in lieu of the father, the mother; and the guardians in lieu of both parents. The guardians of minors (*tutores*) follow the requirements for guardians who function for persons in their majority (*curatores*) in that they may be appointed by the ordinary or, if appointed by the civil law, may be approved by the ordinary for the exercise of the ecclesiastical rights of their wards.[64] The term *minors* varies in meaning with the matter under consideration. In temporal matters, minors are under the power of their parents or guardians until they have attained their majority. In spiritual matters or in matters which have a spiritual connection over which the Church has a proper and exclusive right to judge,[65] however, minors below the age of seven, that is, *infantes*, lack all procedural capacity, inasmuch as they are not bound to the observance of ecclesiastical law,[66] and must be represented in court by their parents or guardians. Minors who are between the ages of seven and fourteen and who enjoy the use of reason also lack procedural capacity, but may act through a guardian given to them by the ordinary or through a proxy chosen by themselves and approved by the ordinary.[67] At the age of fourteen minors receive procedural

[63] F. Roberti, *De Processibus* (4. ed., Romae: Apud Custodiam Librariam Pontificii Instituti Utriusque Iuris, 1956), n. 202.

[64] Cf. canons 1648, § 3; 1651.

[65] Cf. canons 1553, § 1, 1°; 1648, § 3.

[66] Canon 12.

[67] Canon 1648, § 3; Roberti, *op. cit.*, n. 201.

capacity from the law itself without distinction as to sex and can act for themselves thereafter.

Variations of the degree of subjection of minor children to the power of their parents and guardians are also found in the substantive law of the Church. At times parents will exercise the rights of minor children as their legal representatives. This kind of subjection is to be seen in the law concerning the church of funeral and place of burial. Canon 1223, § 1, states the general rule that all who are not prohibited by law may choose the church of their funeral and the place of their burial. The law distinguishes between those who have reached the age of puberty and those who have not reached that age, giving that right to the former and restricting it to the parents or guardians of the latter.[68] A similar provision is made in canon 1456 in which the *ius patronatus,* if it belongs to minors, is exercised for them through their parents or guardians. At other times minors can exercise their rights themselves but require the *consent* of their parents or guardians in order to act *lawfully.* This second degree of subjection of minors to parental authority in the exercise of their rights is seen in canon 1034. In that canon the law charges pastors with the duty of not assisting at the marriages of minors whose parents are either ignorant of the proposed marriage or are *reasonably* unwilling that the marriage take place. The pastor must consult the local ordinary for an appraisal of the reasonableness of the parental opposition. This requirement of law binds under penalty of unlawfulness, but not under pain of invalidity, so that the marriage would be a valid contract, if all other provisions of the law are met, even if the minors married without parental permission or in spite of reasonable parental opposition. At other times minors can exercise their rights without their parents' or guardians' consent. They are obliged to inform their parents or guardians of their intended actions, but may act lawfully even in spite of their opposition. This degree of subjection of minors to parental authority is verified in the law of religious. Canon 538 states that anyone who is a Catholic, who is moved by the right intention, who is bound by no legitimate impediment, and who is

---

[68] Canon 1224, 1°.

judged fit to bear the burdens of religious life may be admitted to religious life. Canon Law demands further that a person be fifteen years of age before he may be validly admitted into the novitiate[69] after a postulancy of at least six months in religious institutes with perpetual vows.[70] Creusen-Ellis[71] note that the Code does not mention the consent of parents as necessary when minors of the age of fourteen make a choice of state of life. Prudence, charity and obedience are recommended in a decision on the part of a minor to enter religious life; nevertheless, the law is silent on this point and, therefore, the right of minors to exercise their rights without the consent of their parents is verifiable in the Code of Canon Law.

### 3. *Moral Persons*

The rights of moral persons in the Code of Canon Law are very much the same as those of physical persons. There are certain rights, however, which are so personal, such as the right to marry or to enter religion, that either by the nature of moral persons or by positive prescript of law moral persons do not possess them.

Among the rights which moral persons do possess are rights which pertain to their status. These rights include the right to the selection and use of their name,[72] the right to the use of the proper insignia and habit,[73] the right of precedence,[74] and the right of juridic domicile.[75]

Other rights may be called patrimonial rights inasmuch as they are concerned with the temporal goods of the Church. In the first place, the Church and moral persons within the Church, independently and freely of the civil government, have the native

---

[69] Cf. canons 542, 1°, and 555, § 1, 1°.

[70] Canon 539.

[71] J. Creusen-A. Ellis, *Religious Men and Women in Church Law* (6. ed., Milwaukee: Bruce Publishing Co., 1958), pp. 141, 142.

[72] Cf. canons 688; 710. These rights are treated at greater length by Michiels, *Principia Generalia de Personis in Ecclesia,* pp. 456-466.

[73] Canon 492, § 3.

[74] Canon 106.

[75] Cf. canons 92; 94, § 1; 1560, 2° and 3°.

right of acquiring, retaining and administering temporal goods for their own spiritual ends.[76] In the second place, the Church and moral persons within the Church have the right of placing juridical acts referring to these temporal goods, such as acts of acquisition, administration and alienation as well as contracts, trusts and debts. These rights are mentioned several times in the Code of Canon Law when it deals with specific institutes.[77]

In addition to personal and patrimonial rights the Church and moral persons within the Church also have extra-patrimonial rights. Among these rights are the right of acquiring incorporeal goods such as rescripts, favors, privileges and indulgences;[78] the right of establishing juridically binding constitutions for themselves;[79] the ability to stand in court, and to enjoy the protection of the law inasmuch as moral persons are considered minors before the law.[80]

One of the ways in which moral persons are restrained in the exercise of their rights is to be found in the law concerning the use of privileges. A privilege may be defined as "a special disposition made by competent authority granting to some person or persons a right which is contrary to or beyond the common law."[81] According to canon 69 no one is obliged to use a privilege which was granted exclusively in his favor, unless there is an obligation to do so on some other ground. The wording and tenor of canon 69 imply that at times a person may be obliged to exercise his right, and to that extent the exercise of his otherwise liberation right is positively restricted.[82] The implication contained in canon 69 is developed in canon 72, which treats of the revocation of privileges. The general principle is stated in the first paragraph, that any private person can renounce a privilege

---

[76] Canon 1495, §§ 1 and 2.

[77] Cf. canons 531; 691; 717, § 2; 1209; 1355; 1409; 1410; and 1489, § 2.

[78] Cf. canons 1495, § 1 and 1497, § 1. Examples are found in canons 36, § 1; 72, §§ 3 and 4; 613, § 1; 615; 708; 1180, etc.

[79] Canons 501, § 1; 410; 689, § 1 and 697, § 1; and 715, § 1.

[80] Canons 1552, § 2, 1°, and 1649 and ff.

[81] Bouscaren-Ellis, *op. cit.*, p. 63.

[82] "Nemo cogitur uti privilegio in sui dumtaxat favorem concesso, nisi alio ex capite exsurgat obligatio."

established exclusively in his favor. If the privilege is granted to a community, dignity or place, it may not be renounced by any private individual. Even the community itself which possesses the privilege may not renounce a privilege if the renunciation would be prejudicial to the Church or to other persons.

Roelker[83] notes that a private person may be obliged to use a privilege when an obligation arises from an extraneous source. He gives the example of a person who enjoys the privilege of attending divine services in an area which is under an interdict. Another reason is the common good together with an imminent private injury which may make the use of a privilege obligatory.[84] Roelker applies the last mentioned reason to the question whether moral persons are bound to use privileges. First he divides privileges into two kinds: those which come from the common law and those which have their source in particular law. Among the former are clerical privileges and clerical exemptions. These privileges must be used because they are conceded to the person in view of his state in life, and also because any personal discomfort which is suffered in the exercise of the privileges would not justify sacrificing the rights of the community. With respect to privileges coming from particular law, there is an obligation that such privileges be used, first, because the privilege belongs to the community and not to the individuals that make it up, and also because continued non-use infringes upon the rights which were obtained by the entire community.[85] This opinion seems to be the common one among contemporary canonists.[86]

A second way in which the rights of moral persons may be restrained is seen in the law pertaining to the appointment of moral persons as pastors of parishes. Canon 451 defines a pastor as a priest or a moral person to whom a parish has been committed

---

[83] *Principles of Privilege according to the Code of Canon Law,* The Catholic University of America Canon Law Studies, n. 35 (Washington, 1926), pp. 94-96.

[84] *Loc. cit.;* Maroto, *op. cit.,* I, n. 300.

[85] Roelker, *op. cit.,* pp. 96-98.

[86] Cicognani, *Canon Law,* p. 805; Michiels, *Normae Generales,* II, 591-593. Michiels holds that the members of the community are bound to use their privileges because of the public good of the community.

in title with the care of souls. The care of souls is to be exercised under the authority of the local ordinary. Canon 1425 describes two ways in which a parish may be committed to the care of religious. The first is effected *pleno iure,* so that the parish becomes a religious parish and the right of the local ordinary is limited to the supervision of what pertains to the care of souls. The second is effected *semi-pleno iure,* so that by an act of the Holy See the parish is united to a religious house only in what pertains to the temporalities of the parish. In this case the parish is still under the care of the local ordinary. The religious superior must choose a *secular* priest to act as pastor.[87] The secular priest must be presented to the local ordinary, who will install him in office. The sustenance of the secular priest so chosen, approved and installed as pastor must by law amount to a suitable portion of the parochial income. Subject to these restrictions the parish is united to the religious house and the moral person of the religious institute; the moral person, moreover, enjoys the right of sharing in a portion of the income of the parish.

A third way in which the rights of moral persons may be restrained at law is found in the law for religious. Canon 497, § 2, states that, when a clerical religious institute receives permission to build a new house, there is also granted to the religious community the faculty of having a church or a public oratory connected with the religious house and of performing liturgical ceremonies in the church or oratory according to the conditions imposed in the permission of the local ordinary. At this point canon 497, § 2, refers to canon 1162, § 4, which gives the local ordinary the right to determine the exact place where the church or oratory is to be built. Canon 1162, § 4, implies a partial restriction of the right of the religious institute. The previous paragraph of the same canon requires that the local ordinary hear the pastors of neighboring churches before giving his consent to the building of a new church. The criteria to be followed in giving or withholding consent are provided in canon 1162, §§ 2 and 3, namely, that it is prudently estimated that financial resources are present for the building and maintenance of a church and that the

[87] Canon 1425, § 1.

harm that befalls already existing neighboring parishes will be outweighed by the provision of greater spiritual service to the faithful. The third paragraph of canon 1162 reminds the neighboring pastors and the local ordinary of the right, provided in canon 1676, of denouncing a new work or enterprise to a judge because of the damage which is feared if the work is allowed to be begun or continued. The protest asks that the work be interrupted until the respective rights of the parties at suit are definitely adjudicated by the court. The party that intends to undertake or has begun to undertake a new work, in this instance the clerical religious institute which wishes to build a church or a public oratory, once that party is informed of the prohibition, must cease his work at once.[88] The local ordinary and/or the neighboring pastors must show cause within two months after having made the denunciation why the work should not be allowed to continue. This time limit may be lengthened or shortened by the judge, for a good and necessary cause, after hearing the other party. In either event the controlling factor will be the common good of the Church as a whole. It is the opinion of the writer, therefore, that, no matter what the outcome of the litigation, the right of the clerical religious institute is restricted when it is demonstrated that its exercise would work against the common good of the Church.

## B. Persons Enjoying Less Than Full Membership in the Church

Canon 87 makes reference to baptized Christians whose rights are restricted because, in the words of the canon, they have placed an *obex* or obstacle which impedes the bond of communion. The obstacle mentioned pertains to the exercise of rights.[89] This *obex* is verified in adults who formally and externally profess heresy, apostasy or schism. But even if adults who profess heresy, schism

[88] Canon 1676, § 2, allows the party against whom the protest is lodged to ask the judge if he may proceed with the work provided he can give security that he can restore everything to its former condition if he should lose the case.

[89] Bouscaren-Ellis, *Canon Law, A Text and Commentary,* pp. 26, 27, and Cicognani, *Canon Law,* p. 570, both hold that an *obex* does not excuse from the observance of ecclesiastical laws, but ignorance on the part of persons in good faith may not hold them to their observance.

or apostasy were in good faith, that is, materially and externally, they too are impeded from the bond of communion with the Church here on earth. The reason is that they are separated from the Church at least in the external forum. Conversely, this *obex* is not found in adults professing heresy, apostasy or schism internally or occultly. The reason here is that there is no bond in the internal forum and, furthermore, the law looks only to the external forum of provable acts. Neither is the obstacle to communion to be found in infants who have not yet reached the age of presumptive use of reason because generally they are not bound to the observance of ecclesiastical law.

The restriction of rights contained in canon 87 is generic, and one must look to individual instances in the Code of Canon Law for a development of the principle. It should be pointed out, nonetheless, that the baptized, whether formal or material heretics, apostates, schismatics or excommunicates, possess some rights in the Church. At the very least, these subjects of the Church have the right to those things which are necessary for them to attain their end, namely, salvation.[90] The reason comes from the nature of the church which has been established not as an end in itself but which exists for the good of its members.

An analysis of the status of each of these categories lies beyond the scope of this dissertation. It will be of interest, however, to define each category of person and to list the major rights which are restricted in the Code of Canon Law.

### 1. *Heretics*

A heretic is any baptized Christian who, while he remains a Christian, denies or positively doubts a truth of the Faith which

---

[90] "Necessaria cum sit Ecclesia, homines morali tenentur obligatione eandem ingrediendi ac, membra eius semel facta, iuridica seu canonica adstringuntur obligatione eiusdem praescripta observandi. *Medium iis necessarium cum sit, eius membra ad ea semper ius habent subiectivum sine quibus finem individualem necessario attinendum assequi non valent.* Ecclesiae praecise est haec necessaria fidelibus praestare iura atque horum iurium possessionem debita tutela tutam reddere."—W. Onclin, "art. cit.," pp. 20, 21; Michiels, *Principia Generalia de Personis in Ecclesia*, p. 27. (Writer's italics.)

is to be believed with divine and catholic faith.[91] Among the effects of the simple delict of heresy there are certain effects which entail the loss or restriction of rights. The Code of Canon Law lists these effects as: the exclusion from the communion of the faithful (canon 2257); the acquisition of the legal status of *toleratus* (canon 2258); the loss of the right to assist at divine services, except the preaching of the word of God (canon 2259); the loss of the right to receive the sacraments (canon 2260); the loss of the right to administer actively the sacraments and sacramentals, except in the special cases mentioned in the law (canon 2261); the loss of the right to perform authorized ecclesiastical acts, to be a plaintiff in ecclesiastical courts, to fulfill ecclesiastical functions and offices, and to enjoy privileges previously granted by the Church (canon 2263); the loss of the right to perform acts of jurisdiction (canon 2264); the loss of the right to share in the election of persons to ecclesiastical offices, the right of being appointed thereto, or the right to receive Holy Orders (canon 2265).[92]

## 2. *Apostates*

An apostate is one who has totally withdrawn from the Christian faith.[93] Some of the rights which are restricted in the case of apostasy are the right of receiving Holy Orders,[94] the right of ecclesiastical burial,[95] and the right of patronage.[96]

---

[91] "Post receptum baptismum si quis, nomen retinens christianum pertinaciter aliquam ex veritatibus fide divine et catholica credendis denegat aut de ea dubitet, haereticus [est] . . ."—Canon 1325, § 2.

[92] E. F. MacKenzie, *The Delict of Heresy,* The Catholic University of America Canon Law Studies, n. 77 (Washington, 1932), p. 44; W. J. Tierney, *Authorized Ecclesiastical Acts,* The Catholic University of America Canon Law Studies, n. 414 (Washington, D. C.: The Catholic University of America Press, 1961), pp. 60, 61.

[93] ". . . si a fide christiana totaliter recidit, apostata [est] . . ."—Canon 1325, § 2.

[94] Canon 985, 1°.

[95] Canon 1240, § 1, 1°.

[96] Canons 1453, § 1, and 1470, § 1, 6°.

### 3. *Schismatics*

A schismatic is a person who refuses to acknowledge the primacy and supremacy of the Roman Pontiff or to associate with members of the Church who do acknowledge that primacy and supremacy.[97] Schismatics are treated by the law in much the same way as heretics with regard to those rights which are restricted because of the *obex* which is incurred when the bond of communion is broken in the external forum.[98]

### 4. *Excommunicates*

It will be recalled that juridic personality in the Church is established through valid baptism with water. For those who enjoy the use of reason there are the added requirements of the profession of faith and the bond of communion. When anyone, whether knowingly (formally) or unknowingly (materially), denies a truth of the Faith which is to be believed with divine and catholic faith he is within the framework of the law a heretic. One who refuses to submit to the primacy and supremacy of the Roman Pontiff, that is, one who breaks the bond of communion, is a schismatic. Canon 87 lists these requirements for the acquisition of juridic personality in the Church separately and antecedently to any consideration of those who separate themselves from full membership in the Church by censure.[99] This manner of speaking of canon 87 distinguishes between those who have separated themselves from full membership in the Church without

---

[97] ". . . si denique subesse renuit Summo Pontifici aut cum membris Ecclesiae ei subiectis communicare recusat, schismaticus est."—Canon 1325, § 2.

[98] Canons 167, § 1, 4°; 731, § 2; 765, 2°; 795, 2°; 795, 2°; 985, 1°; 1453, § 1; 1470, § 1, 6°; 1240, § 1, 1°. Cf. also Michiels, *Principia Generalia de Personis in Ecclesia,* p. 25.

[99] A censure is defined in canon 2241, § 1, as a penalty by which a person who is baptized, who has committed a crime, and who is contumacious, is deprived of certain spiritual goods, or of goods which are attached to spiritual ones, until, having desisted from contumacy, he is absolved."—Bouscaren-Ellis, *Canon Law,* p. 880. Canon 2255, § 1, lists the kinds of censure as excommunication, interdict and suspension. Cf. Bouscaren-Ellis, *op. cit.,* p. 896.

delictual imputability and those whose separation from full membership in the Church as regards the acquisition of, possession of and exercise of their rights results from criminal activity which is subject to an ecclesiastical penalty. It is because of this distinction in canon 87 that the two categories are considered separately, even though, from the point of view of penal law, they are connected. The point is that, although the causes for separation from full membership in the Church may be different, nevertheless, their effects may be the same. Thus it follows that the law determines the same penalties for those who are excommunicated for the commission of delicts other than heresy with the same loss and restriction of rights as for those who are excommunicated because they have committed the delict of heresy.

### 5. *Other Censures*

The Church in the penal law of the Code restricts rights in different ways. Besides the penalty of excommunication there are the penalties of interdict and suspension and the juridic conditions of infamy of law and infamy of fact.

The nature and effects of an interdict are stated quite succinctly by Cloran:

> An interdict is a censure by which the faithful, while remaining in communion with the Church, are forbidden the use of certain sacred things which are enumerated in the canons which follow (canon 2268, § 1). The prohibition is imposed either directly by a *personal,* when the use of things is forbidden to the persons themselves, or indirectly by a *local* interdict, when their dispensation or reception is forbidden in certain places (canon 2268, § 2). The things forbidden by interdict are liturgical services, some of the sacraments, and Christian burial, but not preaching. Since interdict is usually a medicinal penalty, it is called a censure, but at times it may be a vindictive penalty, as when it is imposed for a definite time (cf. canon 2255, § 2).[100]

[100] O. M. Cloran, *Previews and Practical Cases, Code of Canon Law, Book Five: Delicts and Penalties* (Milwaukee: Bruce Publishing Co., 1951), p. 185; Bouscaren-Ellis, *Canon Law,* p. 842; Regatillo, *op. cit.,* II, n. 1028; E. Conran, *The Interdict,* The Catholic University of America Canon Law Studies, n. 56 (Washington, D. C., 1930), pp. 1-9.

Those who are personally interdicted may not exercise the right of electing, presenting or nominating someone to an ecclesiastical office. Neither may such persons obtain dignities, offices, benefices, ecclesiastical pensions or any other function in the Church. Neither may such persons be promoted to Holy Orders.[101]

A suspension is a censure which is applied only to clerics; it restricts them with reference to the rights attaching to an office a benefice, or both. The effects of a suspension are separable, but a general suspension includes suspension from office and from benefice.[102]

Suspension from office forbids any act of the power of orders, of jurisdiction, and of administration which belongs to an office, except the administration of the property pertaining to one's own benefice.[103] Canon 2279, § 2, lists nine different kinds of suspension from office: *suspensio a iurisdictione,* which forbids every act of jurisdiction for both fora, whether ordinary or delegated; *suspensio a divinis,* which forbids every act of the power of orders which one receives either from Holy Orders or by way of privilege; *suspensio ab ordinibus,* which forbids every act of orders received from ordination; *suspensio a certo et definito ordine exercendo,* which forbids the exercise of every act of the order designated, the conferral of the same order by the suspended party, the reception of higher orders by the suspended party, and the exercise of the received order after the suspension takes effect; *suspensio a sacris ordinibus,* which forbids every act of the power of orders received through ordination to Holy Orders, that is, major orders: *suspensio a certo et definito ordo conferendo,* which forbids the conferral of the order under suspension but not the conferral of lower or higher orders; *suspensio a certo et definito ministerio,* which forbids such things as the hearing of confessions, etc., *vel officio,* such as the *cura animarum,* so that every act of parochial or diocesan ministration or office which involves the care of souls is forbidden; *suspensio ab ordine pontificali,* which forbids every act of the power of the episcopal order; and

---

[101] Canons 2275 and 2265.

[102] Canon 2278, §§ 1 and 2.

[103] Canon 2279, § 1.

*suspensio a pontificalibus,* which forbids the exercise of the pontifical acts according to canon 337, § 2, that is, the use of the crozier and mitre.[104]

A *suspensio a beneficio* deprives one of the right to the fruits of the benefice, except the right to live in the house belonging to it, but not of the right to administer the property of the benefice, unless the decree or sentence of suspension expressly takes this power away from the suspended cleric and gives it to another.[105]

Canon 2285 deals with suspension lodged against a collective body. If a community or college, that is, a moral person in the Church, has committed a delict, suspension can be imposed upon the individual guilty persons or upon the community as such. In the latter case, the community is forbidden to exercise the spiritual rights which belong to it as a community.

Besides the already mentioned penalties which effectively restrain the free exercise of rights, the Code of Canon Law makes provision for the penalty of legal infamy (*infamia iuris*).[106] Fame or good repute is the approved estimation of oneself in the judgment of prudent and upright men.[107] Infamy is the loss of fame or good repute. This loss is called infamy of law when it is brought about by the commission of a grave offense to which the law has applied infamy as a penalty. The Code of Canon Law lists the specific effects of infamy at law. The infamous person is irregular according to canon 984, 5°. This last mentioned canon renders a person unable (*inhabilis*) to receive Holy Orders, until he is dispensed from the irregularity, who has either mutilated himself or others or who has attempted to commit suicide. Likewise the infamous person is incapable of obtaining ecclesiastical benefices; he is disqualified from receiving ecclesiastical offices,

---

[104] Canon 2279, § 2, 1°-9°.

[105] Canon 2280, § 1; Bouscaren-Ellis, *Canon Law,* p. 904; Cloran, *Delicts and Penalties,* pp. 190, 191; E. G. Rainer, *Suspension of Clerics,* The Catholic University of America Canon Law Studies, n. 111 (Washington, D. C., 1937), pp. 58-112, where the author treats of the effects of suspension at great length.

[106] Canon 2293, § 1.

[107] "Existimatio est dignitatis inlaesae status legibus et moribus comprobatus . . ."—D.(50.13)5, 1.

dignities or pensions, as well as from performing authorized ecclesiastical acts or from exercising any ecclesiastical right or function; and, finally, he must be prevented from taking part in sacred functions.[108]

Infamy of fact (*infamia facti*) occurs when anyone, because of a crime which he has committed or because of his bad character, has lost his good reputation among serious and prudent practicing Catholics. The decision as to the factual loss of reputation belongs to the ordinary.[109] The effects of infamy of fact are that the person is simply impeded from the reception of Holy Orders while, in the judgment of the ordinary, the person continues to labor under the infamy of fact; that a person is prevented from accepting ecclesiastical dignities, benefices, and offices; that a person is prevented from exercising the sacred ministry, and from the performance of authorized ecclesiastical acts.[110]

---

[108] Canon 2294, § 1; V. A. Tatarczuk, *Infamy of Law*, The Catholic University of America Canon Law Studies, n. 357 (Washington, D. C.: The Catholic University of America Press, 1954), pp. 66-89; Cloran, *Delicts and Penalties*, pp. 218, 219; Bouscaren-Ellis, *Canon Law*, pp. 914, 915; W. J. Tierney, *op. cit.*, pp. 98-101. E. Regatillo, *Institutiones Iuris Canonici* (2 vols., 5. ed., Santander: Sal Terrae, 1956), II, n. 946 touches upon the manner in which the penalty is to be meted out. A *ferendae sententiae* penalty takes away every right that the guilty party has to his good name after the sentence has been enacted. A *latae sententiae* penalty does not take away the right of the guilty party to his reputation until a declaratory sentence has been delivered. The *latae sententiae* penalty does indeed by virtue of canon 2232, § 1, bind the delinquent antecedently to the sentence, but the delinquent is excused from the observance of the penalty bcause of his right to his good name before the deliverance of the declaratory sentence. He would, however, be bound to the observance of the penalty if the delict and its perpetrator became notorious.

[109] Canon 2293, § 3.

[110] Canon 2294, § 2; Regatillo, *loc. cit.;* Bouscaren-Ellis, *loc. cit.;* W. J. Tierney, *op. cit.*, pp. 127-132; F. J. Rodimer, *The Canonical Effects of Infamy of Fact*, The Catholic University of America Canon Law Studies, n. 353 (Washington, D. C.: The Catholic University of America Press, 1954), p. 119.

# CHAPTER VII

## The Restraint of the Exercise of One's Rights in the Code of Canon Law

It will be recalled that the Church has the constitutional and legal right of restricting the exercise of the rights of its members whenever the exercise of these rights would interfere with the attainment of the Church's mission. The Church has categorized its members into different groups whose juridic status differs according to age and the use of reason. These members are more or less free in the exercise of their rights, but the Church, like the civil society, protects its members from unreasonable and imprudent actions when these actions jeopardize the personal rights of their agents or when these actions enter the social sphere and no longer remain private actions. The previous chapter indicated the criteria used by the Church in restraining the exercise of rights, both from the point of view of the subject whose rights were restrained and from the point of view of the rights which were the object of the restraint. It will be the purpose of this chapter to select several instances in the substantive and procedural law of the Church wherein the exercise of rights is expressly restrained.

It should be borne in mind that this chapter is not intended to be an exhaustive treatment of all the canons which restrict the exercise of rights; neither is it an attempt to provide a complete canonical commentary on the individual canons. Rather it will serve to indicate certain particular canons which restrain the free exercise of one's rights, how these rights are restrained, and for what purpose they are restrained.

### SECTION I. THE LAW OF PERSONS AND THINGS

#### *Article 1. The Right of a Religious to Receive the Sacrament of the Holy Eucharist*

The substantive law of the Code of Canon Law contains a restriction of the ability of a religious subject to exercise his right of receiving Holy Communion in canon 595, § 3.[1] This paragraph of canon 595 is a derogation from the general law of the Church concerning the reception of this Sacrament and, since it is a restriction of the exercise of rights, it must be strictly interpreted.[2]

Canon 853 states that any baptized person who is not prohibited by law has the right to receive the Holy Eucharist.[3] The positive prescriptions of the law that a person must possess sufficient use of reason to understand the Real Presence of Christ in the Eucharist and the nature and effects of the Sacrament of Penance are contained in canon 854. The judgment as to an individual's fitness to receive the Holy Eucharist rests with the confessor and the child's parents or guardians. In the exceptional case of danger of death, the sole requirement of the law is that the recipient be able to distinguish the Holy Eucharist from common food and adore Christ in the Real Presence. Canon 855 forbids the reception of Holy Communion by those who are publicly unworthy, that is, by excommunicates, the interdicted, and the manifestly infamous unless such persons have repented, have done penance and have repaired whatever public scandal may have arisen. Canon 856 reminds Christians that no one whose conscience is burdened with grave sin may receive Holy Communion without first receiving the Sacrament of Penance. This prohibition is true no matter how contrite of heart the person may consider himself. The law provides for the exceptional case in which necessity urges the reception of Holy Communion and there is no opportunity of confessing one's sins. In this exceptional case the law requires a person to elicit an act of perfect contrition before receiving the Holy Eucharist. Canon 857 permits one to receive Holy Communion but once in a day except in danger of death. Finally, canon 858, § 1, forbids one from receiving the Holy Eucharist

---

[1] "Si autem post ultimam sacramentalem confessionem religiosus communitati gravi scandalo fuerit aut gravem et externam culpam patraverit, donec ad paenitentiae sacramentum denuo accesserit, Superior potest eum, ne ad sacram communionem accedat, prohibere."

[2] Canon 19.

[3] "Quilibet baptizatus qui iure non prohibetur, admitti potest et debet ad sacram communionem."

who has not fulfilled the conditions of the Eucharistic fast.[4] Outside of these prohibitions the general law of the Church is that any baptized person has the right of receiving the Sacrament of the Holy Eucharist as frequently as once a day.

Canon 595 addresses itself to religious superiors on the matter of the spiritual obligations of their subjects. The first two paragraphs are exhortatory in nature since they are dealing with personal obligations of religious and the supervisory role of the superior in the fulfillment of these obligations on the part of the subjects. The first paragraph lists the various duties of religious: yearly retreat, daily meditation, assistance at daily Mass, private devotions according to the rule or constitutions of the community, and confession at least weekly. The second paragraph instructs superiors to promote the frequent and even daily reception of Holy Communion; this exhortation, however, must leave the subjects free to receive or not to receive this Sacrament.[5] The Church is most insistent that this freedom of conscience and of action be preserved; furthermore, the fourth paragraph of the same canon guarantees this freedom to all religious whose rules or constitutions specify that Holy Communion be received on stated days. Such rules have no coercive force and bind only as suggestions of private devotions.[6]

The third paragraph of canon 595, however, confers upon the superior the right and the power of forbidding anyone of his subjects to receive the Holy Eucharist until the subject has first received the Sacrament of Penance. The superior enjoys this power when the subject has committed a grave and external crime

---

[4] The law of the Code required fasting from both food and water from midnight (*a media nocte*) of the day on which one was to receive the Holy Eucharist. This canon was modified by the Apostolic constitution *Christus Dominus* issued by Pope Pius XII on January 6, 1953—*AAS,* XLV (1953), 15 ff.; *CLD,* IV, 269-282. The law was further simplified by Pope Pius XII in the motu proprio *Sacram Communionem* which was issued on March 19, 1957—*AAS,* XLIX (1957), 177 ff.; *CLD,* IV, 286-288.

[5] The Sacred Congregation of the Sacraments issued a reserved instruction on December 8, 1938, on daily Communion and the precautions to be taken against abuses. Cf. *CLD,* II, 208-212.

[6] ". . . hae normae vim dumtaxat directivam habet."—Canon 595, § 4.

and/or has given grave scandal to the community.[7] These two conditions may be present together but need not be. In any event, the superior possesses the power to forbid the reception of Holy Communion.[8]

Authors differ on the interpretation of these two conditions and the function of the prohibition. Schaefer[9] holds that grave and external faults are to be considered in the strict sense, that is, in the sense that these sins must be submitted to the power of the keys according to the prescription of canon 901.[10] Another reason for the strict interpretation is that the law is dealing with a *res odiosa* in canon 595, § 3. This reason is advanced by Schaefer even though he maintains that the third paragraph of canon 595 contains a penalty not in the sense of canon 2215,[11] that is, a deprivation of some good for the correction of the delinquent, from which recourse may be had *in suspensivo* according to canon 2287,[12] but in the sense of a penal precept from which recourse may be had *in devolutivo tantum* according to canon 345 at the time of the episcopal visitation.[13]

---

[7] Examples of grave scandal are given by some authors. Among the examples are open disobedience, fighting, complete drunkenness even if not seriously sinful in the internal forum. Cf. Beste, *Introductio in Codicem,* p. 434; Vermeersch-Creusen, *Epitome Iuris Canonici,* I, 567, n. 751; F. Claeys-Bouuaert and G. Simenon, *Manuale Juris Canonici,* I, 401, n. 663.

[8] P. M. Clancy, *The Local Religious Superior,* The Catholic University of America Canon Law Studies, n. 175 (Washington, D. C.: The Catholic University of America Press, 1943), p. 99; R. E. McGrath, *The Local Superior in Non-Exempt Clerical Congregations,* The Catholic University of America Canon Law Studies, n. 351 (Washington, D. C.: The Catholic University of America Press, 1954), p. 83.

[9] *De Religiosis* (3. ed., Romae: Herder, 1940), pp. 704, 705, n. 341.

[10] "Qui post baptismum mortalia perpetravit, quae nondum per claves Ecclesiae directe remissa sunt, debet omnia quorum post diligentem sui discussionem conscientiam habeat, confiteri et circumstantias in confessione explicare, quae speciem peccati mutent."

[11] "Poena ecclesiastica est privatio alicuius boni ad delinquentis correctionem et delicti punitionem a legitima auctoritate inflicta."

[12] "Ab inflictis poenis vindicativis datur appellatio seu recursus in suspensivo, nisi aliud expresse in iure caveatur." Cf. T. J. Bowe, *The Power of Religious Superioresses,* The Catholic University of America Canon Law Studies, n. 228 (Washington, D. C.: The Catholic University of America Press, 1946), p. 81.

[13] Schaefer, *op. cit.,* p. 229, § 107.

The opinion of Schaefer has some merit but under close scrutiny it suffers from certain defects. In the first place, if a grave and external sin were required according to the meaning of canon 901, that is, necessary matter for the Sacrament of Penance, the subject would be prevented from receiving Holy Communion according to canon 595, § 3, just as he would be prevented by canon 856[14] except in the case of necessity. In the light of canon 856 it is difficult to explain the need of canon 595, § 3, if grave and external violations are required for the conferral of the power of prohibition upon the superior. In the second place the law preceding the Code of Canon Law expressed a different purpose. Canon 595, § 3, is almost a verbatim repetition of the preceding legislation.[15] The previous legislation expressed the purpose of the law, namely, "to foster the spiritual advancement of religious subjects and to preserve peace, unity and concord in religious communities."[16] According to canon 6, 2°,[17] this decree may be used in the interpretation of canon 595, § 3. Therefore, the law of canon 575, § 3 is more a disciplinary law than a penal law because its purpose, as expressed in previous legislation, is to ensure the discipline of the community and to foster a charitable spirit in the community. In the third place, if one were to follow the opinion of Schaefer, one is placed in

---

[14] "Nemo quem conscientia peccati mortalis gravat, quantumcumque etiam se contritum existimet, sine praemissa sacramentali confessione ad sacram communionem accedat; quod si urgeat necessitas ac copia confessarii illi deest, actum perfectae contritionis prius eliciat."

[15] The decree *Quemadmodum* of the S. C. of Bishops and Regulars issued on December 17, 1890, treats of the permission of receiving Holy Communion. The Holy See says such a permission or prohibition looks only to the ordinary or extraordinary confessor. Superiors have no power of interfering, ". . . excepto casu quo quis ex eorum subditis post ultimam sacramentalem confessionem communitati scandalo fuerit, aut gravem externam culpam patraverit, donec ad Poenitentiae sacramentum denuo accesserit."—*Fontes,* n. 2017.

[16] ". . . ad spiritualem alumnorum profectum et ad unitatis pacem et concordiam in Communitatibus servandam fovendamque. . . ."—*Loc. cit.* (Writer's translation.)

[17] "Canones qui ius vetus ex integro referunt, ex veteris iuris auctoritate, atque ideo ex receptis apud probatos auctores interpretationibus sunt aestimandi. . . ."

the position of discerning and judging objective moral guilt in an individual religious. Such judgments pertain to the internal forum and deal with the subjective dispositions of the individual. This manner of acting is contrary to the spirit of the law which concerns itself with external acts. Therefore, it is the opinion of the writer that the grave scandal and the external fault as mentioned in canon 595, § 3, is only that which interferes very noticeably with the discipline of the religious house, even though the culprit is not guilty of grave sin, or of any sin at all for that matter. The prescription of canon 595, § 3, is, therefore, a restriction upon the exercise of the right of a religious to receive Holy Communion and is allowable by the law under the circumstances indicated in the canon for the common good of the religious community.

### *Article 2. Irregularities and Impediments*

The Code of Canon Law treats of irregularities and impediments as negative restrictions of freedom of action in the law pertaining to the reception of the Sacraments of Holy Orders and of Marriage. The purpose of this article is to set down the manner in which the rights of a person are effectively restrained by these institutes.

#### A. Holy Orders

It is stated in canon 968, § 1, that the subject capable of the valid reception of Holy Orders is a baptized man. The same canon adds that the subject of Holy Orders must possess the qualities that are required by canon 974, § 1,[18] and be free from any irregularity or impediment. With respect to those who have already received Holy Orders, the second paragraph of canon 968 declares that any person who is affected with an irregularity or

[18] These qualities are listed as: (1) proof of the reception of the Sacrament of Confirmation; (2) possession of moral qualities suited for the reception of Holy Orders; (3) canonical age; (4) requisite knowledge; (5) reception of lower orders; (6) observance of the interstices; and (7) canonical title in the case of major orders. The requirements for episcopal consecration are listed in canon 331.

impediment, even though the irregularity or impediment is incurred after ordination, is forbidden to exercise the orders which he has received. It also declares that the same provision applies equally to those who have incurred the irregularity or impediment without any fault on their part as well as to those who have culpably incurred such irregularity or impediment.

It should be pointed out that no one has a right to receive Holy Orders until he is canonically called to the reception of orders by the bishop. This teaching is explicitly found in Holy Scripture[19] and in the statements of the early Fathers.[20] Saint Pius X (1903-1914) confirmed this teaching when he approved the decision of the Commission of Cardinals of June 26, 1912, commending to the faithful the book of Canon Joseph Lahitton entitled *La vocation sacerdotale*. A major tenet of that book was the thesis that no one has any right to receive Holy Orders before he has received the call of the bishop.[21] The call of the bishop as well as the possession of the moral, intellectual and physical prerequisites as set forth in canons 973 and 974 plus the interior subjective call from God Himself qualify a person for the reception of Holy Orders. Thus it happens that the Code of Canon Law speaks never in terms of an objective right to Holy Orders previous to their reception but only of the right to the exercise of orders which have already been received.

An irregularity may be defined as a perpetual impediment or obstacle established by ecclesiastical law because of the reverence which is due to the divine ministry. An irregularity prohibits primarily the reception of Holy Orders and secondarily the exercise of orders received.[22] Irregularities have a twofold source;

---

[19] Hebrews 5:6; John 10:1; John 15:16; Luke 10:2; Acts 1:24.

[20] St. Leo the Great (440-461), *Sermo III*, n. 1—MPL, LIV, 145; St. Gregory the Great (590-604), *Liber Regulae Pastoralis*, Pars I, c. 1—*MPL*, LXXVII, 14.

[21] *Epistola Secretariatae Status ad R.P.D. Carolum M.A. De Cormont, Episcopum Aturensem*, 2 iulii, 1912—*AAS*, IV (1912), 485.

[22] F. M. Cappello, *Tractatus Canonico-Moralis de Sacramentis* (5 vols., Vols. I, II, V, 6. ed.; III, IV, 3. ed., Taurini: Marietti, 1949-1953), IV, n. 435; Beste, *op. cit.*, p. 559; J. J. Hickey, *Irregularities and Simple Impediments*, The Catholic University of America Canon Law Studies, n. 7 (Washington, 1920), p. 9; Vermeersch-Creusen, *op. cit.*, II, 172.

they come into being through a defect in the subject of Holy Orders or through a delict committed by him.[23] It makes no difference whether the person is or is not aware of the irregularity with reference to incurring it. What is necessary is the placing of the action which brings the irregularity into being.[24]

Since a person has no right to receive Holy Orders, there is no question of an irregularity serving as a restriction upon the exercise of his rights. Once a person has received Holy Orders, however, he has an acquired right to exercise them. When a person incurs an irregularity which affects the exercise of his orders, this irregularity constitutes a restriction of the exercise of his rights.

The exercise of orders already received pertains specifically to those acts which are reserved to those persons who have received such orders, and not to each and every act which those in orders may perform. So, for example, clerics in minor orders may perform acts which are permitted to the laity, such as serving Mass, reading in church, opening and closing the church.[25] Some acts are so connected with a certain order that they cannot be placed by one who does not enjoy that order, e.g., to confect the Holy Eucharist or to absolve from sins. These acts are always and necessarily reserved to priests. Other acts of Holy Orders are placed *ex officio* and with special solemnity. Thus the singing of the Epistle at a Solemn Mass, the wearing of the maniple, and the pouring of the water in the chalice are reserved to those who are subdeacons inasmuch as these acts are placed *ex officio* and with that solemnity which is proper to the order. Those persons who are irregular are forbidden to exercise acts of the power of orders which are intimately connected with a special order or which are placed *ex officio* and with solemnity. On the other hand, acts of minor orders are not placed with special solemnity

---

[23] Canon 984 lists seven irregularities which arise from a defect in the subject; canon 985 lists seven irregularities which arise from delicts committed by the subject of Holy Orders.

[24] Canon 988.

[25] Cappello, *op. cit.*, IV, n. 443.

and therefore those who are irregular are not forbidden to exercise those orders.[26]

Among the irregularities listed in the Code of Canon Law only one pertains specifically to the exercise of orders already received, and hence may be considered as a restriction of the exercise of one's rights. Canon 985, 7°, states that clerics in minor orders or laymen who exercise an act of orders reserved to clerics in major orders are irregular. Irregular also are priests, deacons, and subdeacons who exercise an act of orders reserved to clerics in major orders after they have been forbidden to do so by way of a canonical penalty, whether personal, medicinal or vindictive, or local. It is only this irregularity which is incurred by priests, deacons and subdeacons who exercise their orders in violation of a canonical penalty which constitutes a restriction of the exercise of one's rights.

Canon 986 determines the conditions necessary for the incurrence of delictual irregularity as a grave sin, committed after baptism, which is external and to which the irregularity is attached. The delict may be either public or occult. In the case of canon 985, 7°, the specific conditions for incurring the irregularity are: (1) that the act placed must be an act of the power of orders; (2) that the act placed must be an act of the power of sacred orders, that is, an act reserved to clerics who are in major orders; and (3) that the person who places the act either lacks the order or is impeded from its exercise by way of a censure or a vindictive penalty.[27] These conditions must be fulfilled before the irregularity is incurred. Hence it follows that if anyone places an act of the power of orders either inadvertently or upon being lawfully requested by one of the faithful for the exercise of a major cleric's ecclesiastical services, the cleric does not incur the irregularity.[28]

Beyond the restrictive force of the irregularity which is in-

[26] With regard to the order of exorcist, canon 1151 demands that the exorcist receive express and special permission from the bishop before performing an exorcism. The bishop, moreover, is commanded to choose priests who are mature, tried in virtue, and known for their piety, to perform exorcisms.

[27] Cappello, *op. cit.*, IV, n. 509.

[28] Canons 2261, § 2; 2275, 2°; 2284; Cappello, *op. cit.*, IV, n. 511.

curred only upon the fulfillment of all the conditions already mentioned, the law of the Church allows lawful superiors, that is, persons in the Church who have the power to enact laws and to impose precepts, the power of punishing subjects. Because of the scandal given or because of the special gravity attaching to the transgression in a given case, the subject may be punished even without previous warning.[29] The law goes further. It imposes upon the same lawful superior the right and the duty of not promoting to higher orders a cleric of whose fitness he is not certain, and, in order to prevent scandal, of *forbidding a cleric to exercise the sacred ministry,* or even of removing him from office according to law. The lawful superior may act in this manner even though it is only probable that a crime has been committed, or even though penal action against a crime which was certainly committed is now barred in consequence of a favorable legal prescription. These procedures are considered not as penalties,[30] but rather as penal remedies or as penances.[31]

A simple impediment may be defined as a canonical hindrance or obstacle which is of a temporary nature, is established by ecclesiastical law, and of itself prohibits primarily the reception of Holy Orders and secondarily the exercise of the orders received. The most important difference between irregularities and impediments is that the former are permanent by nature and that the latter are temporary by nature. With reference, in general, to the juridical consequences, the effects of the simple impediments are the same as the effects of irregularities.[32]

### B. Marriage

According to canon 1035 every person is free to marry unless he is forbidden to do so by law. The prohibitions by which a

---

[29] Canon 2222, § 1.

[30] Canon 2222, § 2.

[31] Canons 2306-2313.

[32] Cappello, *op. cit.,* IV, n. 449; Vermeersch-Creusen, *op. cit.,* II, 172; Hickey, *op. cit.,* p. 73; H. J. Vogelpohl, *The Simple Impediment to Holy Orders,* The Catholic University of America Canon Law Studies, n. 224 (Washington, D. C.: The Catholic University of America Press, 1945), pp. 3, 4.

person is prevented from entering marriage either validly or lawfully are called impediments. In the strict sense of the term, an impediment is an external circumstance established by divine or human law which either renders a person incapable of entering a marriage contract or restrains him from entering a lawful marriage.[33] The effects of an impediment may be twofold: a diriment impediment prevents a person from entering a valid marriage; an impedient impediment gravely prohibits a marriage to be entered but does not invalidate the contract.[34] An impediment which directly touches only one party affects also the other party, inasmuch as the marriage will be either invalid or unlawful for both parties, depending on the nature of the impediment.[35]

It is evident, then, that the general right of every person to marry, as it is declared in canon 1035, is subject to restrictions in its exercise in consequence of the law enacting the impediments. It is likewise evident that the laws of the Church which pertain to matrimonial impediments, whether diriment or impedient, are to be strictly interpreted according to canon 19, since they contain a restriction of the free exercise of rights.

### *Article 3. The Matrimonial Ban*

The Code of Canon Law very explicitly states that the supreme authority of the Church, that is, the Roman Pontiff, has the unique right of declaring authentically those instances in which the divine law itself forbids marriage under the penalty of either invalidity or unlawfulness.[36] To the same supreme authority of the Church alone belongs the right of establishing impedient and diriment impediments to marriage for the baptized by means of either universal or particular law.[37]

---

[33] Cappello, *op. cit.*, V, n. 195; P. Card. Gasparri, *Tractatus Canonicus de Matrimonio* (2 vols., nova ed., Typis Polyglottis Vaticanis, 1932), I, n. 204; A. DeSmet, *De Sponsalibus et Matrimonio* (2 vols., 4. ed., Brugis, 1927), II, n. 463; J. J. Petrovits, *The New Church Law on Matrimony*, The *Catholic University of America Canon Law Studies*, n. 6 (Philadelphia, 1921), p. 70.

[34] Canon 1036, §§ 1 and 2.

[35] Canon 1036, § 3.

[36] Canon 1038, § 1.

[37] Canon 1038, § 2.

With regard to individual marriages it is also a matter of law that only the Holy See can add to a prohibition an invalidating clause which can prevent any person or, if need be, two persons from entering a valid marriage contract.[38] The Code of Canon Law gives to the local ordinary the power of forbidding any person residing in his territory, and any of his subjects outside his territory, to enter some given marriage. This power, however, extends only to a prohibition under the penalty of unlawfulness, and the conditions which are required for the implementation of this prohibition are very specific. In the first place, the local ordinary can impose the prohibition only in individual instances. In other words, no diocesan policy of universal application may be predicated upon this power. In the second place, the prohibition may be levied upon a couple only for a time, which is more or less definite. It may be given for a month, three months, or six months, as the individual need demands; but a prohibition to marry should not be imposed for a longer period of time when a shorter period of time would manifestly serve the same purpose. In the third place, a just cause is required for imposing the prohibition. The canon explicitly states that the prohibition is effective only as long as there continues in existence the just cause which brought the prohibition into being.[39] Therefore, once the just cause ceases to exist the prohibition also ceases to exist *ipso iure.*

It is evident that the prohibition of the local ordinary is a

---

[38] Canon 1039, § 2.

[39] Canon 1039, § 1. Among the just causes enumerated by authors are the following: (1) the reasonable opposition of parents in the case of the marriage of minors; (2) the suspicion by the pastor or the local ordinary of a hidden impediment, especially a diriment impediment; (2) a warranted fear of scandal; (4) the intention of the sinful abuse of marriage; and (5) the presence of a social disease which is unknown to the other party. Cf. Cappello, *op. cit.,* V, n. 62; Vermeersch-Creusen, *op. cit.,* II, n. 299; De Smet, *op. cit.,* II, n. 486; Gasparri, *op. cit.,* I, n. 230; H. A. Ayrinhac, *Marriage Legislation in the New Code of Canon Law* (revised and enlarged by P. J. Lydon, New York: Benziger Bros., 1957), n. 62; J. M. Waterhouse, *The Power of the Local Ordinary to Impose a Matrimonial Ban,* The Catholic University of America Canon Law Studies, n. 317 (Washington, D. C.: The Catholic University of America Press, 1952), pp. 60-62.

restriction of the exercise of a person's right to marry which is expressed in canon 1035. The purpose of the restriction may be manifold: the prevention or removal of scandal, the prevention of delicts, or the maintenance of the serenity of the social order in general.[40] Because of the nature of marriage both the private good of the individuals and the public good of society must be considered together. It will happen occasionally that the local ordinary will have to restrict the free exercise of the personal rights of individuals in the external forum because of the superseding needs of the ecclesiastical and civil society.

Canon 1039, § 1, since it involves a restriction of the free exercise of one's rights, must be interpreted strictly according to canon 19. At times only the circumstances of the marriage need be restricted: forbidding solemnity and publicity attending the marriage; prohibiting the marriage to take place in a parish or area where the parties are well known, etc. At other times the marriage itself will have to be prohibited until the just cause for the prohibition is removed. According to the principle of canon 19, the lesser restriction should be imposed wherever possible instead of the more rigorous one. At any event, each individual case must be weighed and the decision left to the local ordinary.

### *Article 4. The Juridical Form of Marriage*

The Code of Canon Law declares as a matter of law that only those marriages are valid which are contracted before the pastor, the local ordinary, or a priest delegated by either, and before at least two witnesses.[41] An exception is made for those who are in danger of death or who prudently foresee that a priest will not be available for over a period of one month. In these two exceptional cases the parties may validly and lawfully exchange consent before two witnesses.[42]

It must be pointed out, however, that the general rule of canon 1094 is a restriction of the exercise of one's right to marry as expressed in canon 1035. It follows then that canon 1094 must

---

[40] Waterhouse, *op. cit.*, p. 63.

[41] Canon 1094.

[42] Canon 1098, 1°.

be interpreted strictly, that is, it must be interpreted in such a way that no more people are comprehended under this invalidating prohibition than is necessary through a literal interpretation of its terms.[43]

## SECTION II. THE LAW OF ACTIONS

### *Article 1. The Concept of Rights in Procedural Law*

The procedural law of the Church seeks to protect and to vindicate, if necessary, the rights of its members. This intention is expressed in canon 1646, which states that anyone who is not forbidden by law may undertake a legal action to protect his rights against another party. The other party who is called the defendant must reply to the charge made against him when he has been legitimately cited. The prescription of canon 1646 is subject to some modifications in the succeeding canons of Chapter I of Title IV of Book IV of the Code of Canon Law. Mention has already been made of the restricted procedural capacity of minors and of those who do not enjoy the full use of their reason.[44] To these categories of persons the law adds two more in canon 1652 and 1654. In canon 1652 it is stated that religious do not have, without the consent of their superiors, procedural capacity unless they are vindicating acquired rights which have come to them through religious profession, unless they have legitimately been outside the cloister and the protection of their rights demands the recognition of their procedural capacity, or unless they wish to institute a denunciation of their superior before the law. Canon 1654 allows excommunicates, whether they are *vitandi* or *tolerati,* after a declaratory or condemnatory sentence, to impugn the justice and legitimacy of their excommunication;

---

[43] With the abrogation of the second part of canon 1099, § 2, the law of the Code binds all the validly baptized to the juridical form of marriage. This abrogation was issued by Pope Pius XII in a *motu proprio* on August 1, 1948, and took effect on January 1, 1949.—*AAS,* XL (1948), 305; *CLD,* III, 463, 464. The status of the law regarding the juridical form has been recently criticized by J. C. Barry, "The Tridentine Form of Marriage: Is it Unreasonable?" *The Jurist,* XX (1960), 159-178.

[44] *Supra,* pp. 90-93.

the same canon allows them to act by proxy when they are attempting to avoid anything which would be prejudicial to their spiritual welfare; in other matters they cannot act before the law.

Once it has been determined that a person has a right to stand before the court, the next question is one of right of action: does he have a right which is justiciable at law through an action? Furthermore, what is an action?

Justinian (527-565) defined an action as the right of pursuing in a trial that which is one's due. This definition was a restatement of the thinking of the Roman jurist, Iuventius Celsus,[45] *Nihil aliud est actio quam ius quod sibi debeatur, iudicio persequendi.*[46] This definition has been accepted by canonists[47] as the right of pursuing in a trial that which belongs to a person or that which is due to him.

It is the purpose of the Code of Canon Law to establish in the public forum by positive law those rights which belong to public forum by positive law those rights which belong to persons in the Church by the fact of their membership and also which they have acquired as Christians. Canon 1667 states the general rule that all rights are protected in the positive law by actions which will always be recognized. This statement of canon 1667 provides for express exceptions, however, for there do exist rights which do not enjoy the protection of an action at law. Canon 1017, for instance, states that a promise of marriage which has been made and accepted cannot be enforced in court even though there is evidence that the promise was broken and indeed that it was broken without a reasonable excuse.

With respect to the exercise of rights the law provides protection for them in a petitory action. As a matter of fact canon 1693 grants an action to anyone who possesses a legitimate title to obtain the possession of a certain thing, or the exercise of a

---

[45] Celsus was a respected jurist of the first part of the second century and member of Hadmion's *Consilium.*

[46] D.(44.7)51.

[47] Conte a Coronata, *Institutiones Iuris Canonici*, III, n. 1192; J. Noval, *Commentarium in Codicem Iuris Canonici,* Liber IV, *De Processibus,* Pars I, *De Iuriciis* (Romae, 1920), n. 294 (hereafter cited De Iudiciis); Regatillo, *op. cit.,* II, n. 448.

certain right. Once the action is presented to the court and is fortified with a legitimate title to the exercise of a right, the court must uphold the action. That rights may cede to higher rights is also provided for in the law. The judge must take into consideration the total objective situation and the provisions of the law. If he judges in favor of the plaintiff, he will grant the action.

### *Article 2. The Restraint of the Exercise of One's Rights*

It was stated in the preceding chapter that a person who has juridical capacity in procedural law may undertake a civil action[48] to assert and vindicate his rights. Specifically, he may seek in a petitory action, upon the showing of a proper legal title, the exercise of his rights. The law of incorporeal things, that is, rights and obligations is analogous to the law of things and as a result these petitory actions concerning rights are given in the Code of Canon Law after the fashion of the *actiones utiles*[49] of Roman Law. The lawgiver is accustomed to think in terms of things, that is, quantified matter, and it is difficult to think of rights except in terms of things. This same difficulty is expressed in the law of petitory and possessory actions.[50] This characteristic is verified both in the canons which deal with possessory actions or remedies (canons 1693-1700) and the canons which treat of sequestra-

---

[48] Canon 1552, § 2, 1°, defines a civil, or "contentious," action as one in which persons prosecute or vindicate rights. Paragraph 2, 2°, distinguishes this kind of action from a criminal action, which looks to the infliction or declaration of a penalty.

[49] "These were actions originating through the activity of praetors and jurists by a modification of an already existing formula to cover legal situations and transactions for which the original formula did not suffice. The mechanism of the *actiones utiles* contributed considerably to the development of the law."—*EDRL*, pp. 347, 348, s.v. *actiones utiles;* Schulz, *Classical Roman Law,* pp. 31, 32; Jolowicz, *Historical Introduction to the Study of Roman Law,* pp. 217, footnote 3; 531, 532.

[50] "Qui ad possessionem alicuius rei adipiscendam, *vel ad alicuius iuris exercitium* obtinendum munitur titulo legitimo, petere potest, ut in rei possessionem vel *iuris exercitium* immittatur."—Canon 1693; "Sed in restitutione rei vel *exercitii iuris* aliquod occurrat. . . ."—Canon 1699, § 3. (Writer's italics.)

tion and the restraint of the exercise of one's rights (canons 1672-1675).

Occasionally it will be necessary that a person should be restrained in the exercise of his rights by means of the procedural law of the Church. This subject is treated *ex professo* in Chapter I of Title V of Book IV of the Code of Canon Law under the rubric of sequestration and the restraint of the exercise of one's rights; it is treated incidentally in canon 1699, § 3.

Sequestration was described in the *Digest* as an action whereby a thing which was the subject of controversy was deposited with a third party until the controversy was settled. The third party was called the sequester, because he was, as it were, following the contending parties.[51] In the law of the Decretals sequestration in the proper sense was admitted in exceptional cases.[52] Sequestration in the wide sense pertained to incorporeal rights which were the object of controversy. Three cases of this kind of sequestration are mentioned in the Decretals. The first case concerns a wife who has attacked the validity of her marriage.[53] For certain reasons it is feared that she will be subjected to violence, physical harm, or that she will be sexually attacked by her husband. The court in such circumstances entrusts the safety of her person to an upright woman during the course of the trial. The second case deals with a young girl who is fearful of the unjust influence of

---

[51] D.(50.16)110.

[52] The cases were: (1) If the plaintiff wantonly wasted a thing or its fruits after he had received custody of the thing in controversy by a previous decree, the thing was to be sequestered—c. 2, X, *de sequestratione possessionum et fructuum,* II, 17. (2) If the defendant dissipated the fruits of a controverted thing while awaiting an appeal from a sentence levied against him, the thing was to be sequestered—c. 3, X, *de sequestratione possessionum et fructuum,* II, 17. (3) If a defendant refused contumaciously to appear in court, sequestration of the controverted thing from the defendant's possession was admitted as a means of breaking his contumacy—c. 2, X, *de dolo et contumacia,* II, 14; c. 25, X, *de rescriptis,* I, 3. (4) If a husband were near bankruptcy and it was feared that he might waste his wife's dowry, sequestration was in order to restrain him—c. 7, X, *de feudis,* IV, 20. (5) If a cleric neglected to observe the law of residence, sequestration of the fruits of the benefice was inflicted as a penal remedy until the cleric began to reside in his benefice—c. 28, X, *de appellationibus, recusationibus et relationibus,* II, 28.

[53] Cc. 8, 13, X, *de restitutione spoliatorum,* II, 13.

her parents and relatives in the matter of choosing her state in life.[54] She seeks admittance to a safe place by order of the court so that she can decide without any external interference whether to marry or to enter religious life. The court will grant this request upon the showing of *prima facie* evidence of undue influence. The third case pertains to a religious or someone who is subject to authority and seeks to be removed from that subjection because he rightly fears unjust recriminations on the part of the superior.[55] Sequestration as a means of assuring the custody of property was not known in decretal law, but was favored in the jurisprudence of the Church shortly before the promulgation of the Code of Canon Law.[56]

In the Code of Canon Law sequestration is sometimes inflicted in penal matters as a means of protecting those things which were the object of a crime or had such a connection with a crime that the public good demands their safekeeping in an unaltered condition until the trial, at which time the sequestered things will be produced as evidence. Sequestration is also given as a means of securing one's credit with a creditor in a business transaction.[57] The usual kind of sequestration is that which is called judicial. Judicial sequestration is the depositing of a controverted thing or its fruits with a third party during a lawsuit, so that the thing and its fruits may be restored integrally to the victor of the lawsuit.[58]

---

[54] C. 14, X, *de sponsalibus et matrimoniis,* IV, 1.

[55] C. 14, X, *de probationibus,* II, 19.

[56] The Sacred Roman Rota decided a case of custodianship (*depositum*) from Marseilles on January 25, 1911, in which it prescribed sequestration in the wide sense as a pledge of good faith or as an escrow, and noted that this custodianship was not sequestration in the strict sense "cum haec non respiciat res litigiosas. . . ."—*AAS,* III (1911), 107. The same tribunal was more explicit in a case from Florence concerning burial rights.—*AAS,* VII (1915), 270.

[57] F. Wernz-P. Vidal, *Ius Canonicum* (7 vols. in 8), Tomus VI, *De Processibus* (ed. altera, a F. Cappello recognita, Romae: Apud Aedes Universitatis Gregorianae, 1949), n. 270.

[58] This definition reflects the Roman Law conception of sequestration: "Proprie autem in sequestre est depositum ['quod custodiendum alicui datum est'—D.(16.3)1, pr.] quod a pluribus in solidum certa conditione custodiendum reddendumque traditur."—D.(16.3)6.

Besides sequestration the Code of Canon Law allows the restriction of the exercise of one's rights in canons 1672-1675. This restriction, which in civil law is called an injunction,[59] is a temporary prohibition of the use of a controverted right, which prohibition is lodged against someone by a judge not so much as a penalty but rather as a legal precaution against the danger of injuring the right of another person.[60] The source of the injunction is the power of jurisdiction which the judge enjoys and which he may exercise either in an incidental question which arises during a trial and must be settled before the main issue of the trial can be decided,[61] or as the direct object of the judicial process, or as a declaration of a juridic fact.[62] If the matter is brought to court as a separate litigation an *actio inhibitoria* is entered against him who is exercising his right and is injuring a right of the plaintiff thereby.[63]

The object of the action is the prohibition of the exercise of another's right. Canonists are generally agreed that any right is comprehended in the text of canon 1672, that is, the law allows the restriction of ecclesiastical rights or profane rights. Among the former are included natural and divine law rights which are given protection by Church law and among the latter are those which are protected by civil law and which the plaintiff brings before an ecclesiastical court. As a general rule the ecclesiastical law looks to the protection of ecclesiastical rights, since civil rights factually find protection in the civil courts. The legal basis for the inclusion of civil as well as ecclesiastical rights is the principle that one should not distinguish where the law itself does not distinguish. Canon Law, moreover, accepts the local civil law

---

[59] This institute is referred to by one author as a *decretum de non faciendo* inasmuch as it forbids one to perform a certain act. Cf. M. Lega-V. Bartoccetti, *Commentarius in Iudicia Ecclesiastica iuxta Codicem Iuris Canonici* (3 vols., ed. a V. Bartoccetti, Romae: Azienda Libraria Cattolica Italiana, 1950), I, 392, 393.

[60] J. Noval, *De Iudiciis,* n. 312; Lega-Bartoccetti, *ibid.,* p. 393; Roberti, *op. cit.,* p. 660, n. 239.

[61] Canon 1868.

[62] Canon 1552, § 2, 1°.

[63] Noval, *op. cit.,* n. 313.

of contracts except where Canon Law has enacted its own separate legislation or where the civil law contravenes the natural or positive divine laws.

Lega-Bartoccetti question the application of the restriction of the exercise of rights to the public power of the Church, and specifically to the power of jurisdiction. Does this institute apply as a remedy to the administrative and legislative acts of ordinaries?[64] Does it refer equally to judicial decisions? Lega-Bartocetti[65] answer in the affirmative. The basis of their answer seems to be that these exercises of public power in the Church are as equally subject to the judicial power in the Church as the acts of private individuals, and in a sense even more so because of the added responsibilities of those in whose hands the public power of the Church is entrusted. Another argument would seem to be the reasonableness of the law. The law presumes that reason rests more on one side of an argument than another in a controversy. The point to be made here, however, is that the law is an instrument of reason which operates in such a way as to balance one power with another in an effort to protect the rights and freedom of all in the Church.[66] A third argument is drawn from the previous legislation in which the public power of the Church was subjected to judicial review and was effectively restrained, even though the present remedy was not yet available as a separate and distinct institute.[67]

The conditions which are required by law for the judicial restraint of the exercise of one's rights are set forth in canons

---

[64] Canon 198, § 1.

[65] *Op. cit.*, I, 394.

[66] Although the Church is not a democracy, it is nonetheless true that all Christians have rights in the Church which the law protects according to its terms.

[67] Pope Innocent IV declared in his *Constitutio Romana* that an appeal from a judicial sentence to a higher tribunal included a delay in the execution of the sentence until the appeal was denied, or, if the appeal was granted, until the higher tribunal had definitively rendered sentence. A further consideration of the same constitution was the outcome of prejudicial attempts during the hearing of the appeal. Such attempts were declared to be null and void.—C. 3, *de appellationibus,* II, 15, in VI°; Conc. Trident., sess. XXIV, *de ref.,* c. 20—Mansi, XXXIII, 168, 169.

1672-1675. In the first place, it is required that the party seeking the restriction demonstrate his own right and the loss, harm or injury that would be worked upon him if his neighbor is allowed the exercise of his right.[68] In the second place, it is required that this loss, harm or injury which is feared cannot be avoided in any other way except through the restriction of the exercise of the neighbor's right.[69] The reason for this disposition of the law is found in canon 19, which demands that laws which restrict the free exercise of rights be strictly interpreted. In other words, if the neighbor can prove that the loss, harm or injury which is threatened could otherwise be avoided or repaired, or if the neighbor offered a sum of money as commensurate security against such loss, harm or injury, the restriction cannot be enforced by the judge.[70] In instances in which the public good is involved as well as the private good of the individuals, the action can be granted *ex officio* by the judge or at the request of the promoter of justice especially, or of the defender of the bond.

The judicial restraint of the exercise of one's rights has effects in law. Canon 1854 mentions canons 1672 and 1673 as excepted from the legal notion of an *attentatum lite pendente*.[71] On the other hand, any violation of the judicial restraint of the exercise of one's rights is considered as a prejudicial attempt and the same effects are incurred.[72] Among the effects listed are that any

[68] Canon 1672, §§ 1 and 2.

[69] Canon 1674.

[70] Canon 1674. Cf. Noval, *op. cit.*, n. 318; Roberti, *op. cit.*, p. 663, n. 241; F. Della Rocco, *Canonical Procedure,* translated by John D. Fitzgerald (Milwaukee: Bruce Publishing Co., 1961), pp. 60, 61, n. 32.

[71] An *attentatum* is any attempt during the course of litigation either on the part of one party against another or on the part of the judge against either one or the other party, against which attempt the other party expresses his dissent, or which attempt is prejudical to his rights; this attempt may look either to the matter of the litigation or to the terms assigned to the parties either by law or by the judge for the placing of certain judicial acts. Canon 1854 excepts sequestration and the restraint of the exercise of one's rights from the effects of an *attentatum*. Cf. J. P. Dunnivan, *Prejudicial Attempts in Pending Litigation,* The Catholic University of America Canon Law Studies, n. 379 (Washington, D. C.: The Catholic University of America Press, 1960), pp. 53, 112, 117, 126, 148.

[72] Roberti, *op. cit.*, p. 663, n. 241.

prejudicial attempts during pending litigation are *ipso iure* invalid;[73] that the injured party enjoys an action to obtain a declaration of nullity;[74] that this action must be introduced before the judge of the principal trial, unless the judge is accused of being suspect;[75] that the course of the principal trial is suspended as a rule until the question of a prejudicial attempt is settled;[76] that the question of a prejudicial attempt should be settled as expeditiously as possible by the judge upon hearing the parties, and by the promoter of justice and/or the defender of the bond if they are present in the trial;[77] that, once a prejudicial attempt has been made manifest with moral certainty, the judge must decree its revocation,[78] and, finally, if the prejudicial attempt has been perpetrated by force or by fraud, that the injured party may receive damages from the perpetrator at the direction of the judge.[79]

The law itself gives examples of the judicial restraint of the exercise of one's rights. The first case involves the restitution of the exercise of a right.[80] Though the person deprived of possession when brought to court has the right to be reinstated in possession before the case proceeds, still the judge may at the instance of the other party or of the promoter of justice decree that the reinstatement into the former condition be suspended, or that the object or person be in the custody of the *sequester* until the end of the trial, if there is danger present in the restitution of the thing or of the right—e.g., the danger of cruel treatment of the wife should the man demand the resumption of conjugal relations while the validity of the marriage is being litigated. Another case concerns the use of the right of marital intercourse and even of the necessity of separating the consorts while a marriage is being impugned in an ecclesiastical court.[81] Article 63 of the Instruction of the Sacred Congregation of the Sacraments of August 15, 1936, *Provida*

[73] Canon 1855, § 1.
[74] Canon 1855, § 2.
[75] Canon 1855, § 3.
[76] Canon 1856, § 1.
[77] Canon 1856, § 2.
[78] Canon 1857, § 1.
[79] Canon 1857, § 2.
[80] Canon 1699, § 3.
[81] Roberti, *op. cit.*, p. 663, n. 241.

*Mater,* states that after the tribunal has accepted the *libellus* the tribunal shall order, either at the instance of the promoter of justice or *ex officio,* the separation of the consorts if they should still be living together and if grave scandal exists.[82] A third case is given in Article 223 of the same Instruction. Therein it is ordered that, if either one or both parties should attempt marriage after the nullity of the previous marriage has been affirmatively adjudged in first instance, or even in second instance when an appeal has been lodged by the defender of the bond against the decision, the tribunal *ex officio* or at the request of the same defender of the bond forbid the exercise of the right to marry according to canon 1672, § 3, until a definitive sentence has been delivered. The promoter of justice is also empowered by law to request this restriction of the exercise of a person's right to marry in similar circumstances wherein the public good of the Church demands it. This right and duty of the promoter of justice is not mentioned in Article 223 of the Instruction, but it does receive mention in canon 1672, § 3.[83] In other words, the lawgiver demands that rights which are the subject of litigation may not be exercised; any attempt to exercise such a controverted right will be regarded as an *attentatum,* or prejudicial attempt, according to canon 1854, and will be considered as null and void according to canon 1855, § 1.[84]

### *Article 3. The Restraint of the Exercise of the Right to Impugn a Marriage*

The Code of Canon Law acknowledges the natural right of any

[82] S. C. de Sacramentis, instructio, *Provida Mater,* 15 aug. 1936, Art. 63—*AAS,* XXVIII (1936), 327; W. J. Doheny, *Canonical Procedure in Matrimonial Cases* (2. ed., 2 vols., Milwaukee: Bruce Publishing Co., 1948), I, 205, 206. Doheny notes that, "From the text it is evident that separation of the spouses is not necessary *if scandal is not present,* according to the opinion of the Ordinary."—*Op. cit.,* I, 206. (Writer's italics.)

[83] S. C. de Sacramentis, instructio, *Provida Mater,* 15 aug. 1936, Art. 223—*AAS,* XXVIII (1936), 357; Doheny, *op. cit.,* I, 545, 546. "Sequestratio rei et inhibitio exercitii iuris a iudice decerni potest ex officio, instante praesertim promotore iustitiae aut defensore vinculi, quoties bonum publicum id postulare videatur."—Canon 1672, § 3.

[84] "Attentata sunt ipso iure nulla."—Canon 1855, § 1.

person to contract a marriage when not forbidden by law to do so.[85] This right to contract marriage is protected by canon 1667, which affords an action at court for any right which is granted by positive law, unless the positive law has specifically prohibited such an action.[86] Canon 1679 states, moreover, that, if an act or contract is invalid by law, the party concerned has a right to sue in court for the declaration of its nullity.[87] An act is to be declared null and void, according to canon 1680, § 1, either when the essential constituents of the act are wanting, or when there are not present some formalities or conditions which the law requires under pain of nullity. The party who is laboring under an ineffectual contract may thus seek to have his rights adjudicated in an ecclesiastical court.[88] Canon 1646 provides that any person who is not forbidden by law is able to institute a suit as plaintiff. The principles of the aforementioned canons are brought together and applied in canon 1971, § 1, 1°. Canon 1971, § 1, 1°, enables the spouses to impugn the validity of their marriage as a matter of right, unless they are forbidden by law to do so.[89] The right to bring an action which in an ecclesiastical court impugns the validity of a marriage is immediately dependent upon canon 1667, and ultimately dependent upon canon 87, which restricts the exercise of rights in ecclesiastical law to those validly baptized persons alone who are impeded from the bond of communion with the Catholic Church through heresy, schism, or any ecclesiastical censure.

With respect to the right of a person to impugn the validity of his marriage, those persons who are validly baptized in the Catholic Church, or who have been converted to the Catholic Church, and have not apostatized from the Catholic Faith, that

---

[85] "Omnes possunt matrimonium contrahere, qui iure non prohibentur."—Canon 1035.

[86] "Quodlibet ius . . . actione munitur, nisi aliud expresse cautum sit . . ." —Canon 1667.

[87] "Si actus aut contractus sit ipso iure nullus, datur ei, cuius interest, actio ad obtinendam a iudice declarationem nullitatis."—Canon 1679.

[88] Canon 1552, § 1.

[89] Canon 1971, § 1, 1°, provides for the possible seeking of a separation as well as for the possible impugning of the marriage.

is, those persons who have maintained the bond of communion, enjoy this right. Non-Catholics do not enjoy this right either because they have not maintained the bond of communion, if they are validly baptized, or because they are not baptized at all. This juridic philosophy of personality which is rooted in canon 87 is reflected in documents from the Holy See.[90] It should be pointed out, however, that the Holy Office grants permission in individual cases for an accusation to be made by a non-Catholic plaintiff when the public good of the Church would be of interest. If the public good demands that the accusation be made, the promoter of justice is empowered by canon 1791, § 1, 2°, to make the accusation.[91]

The point at issue, however, is that canon 1971, § 1, 1°, is a restriction of the exercise of one's rights. This conclusion is to be derived from the nature of the law of the canon itself. Canon 1971, § 1, 1°, is an incapacitating law in the sense of canon 11, namely it renders the person unable to act. An invalidating law is one which by positive enactment renders null and void an act which would otherwise be considered as valid and effective. Canon 1094 is an example of an invalidating law, for it prescribes that a couple exchange their marriage vows in the presence of the pastor, the local ordinary, or a priest delegated by either of them, and before at least two witnesses, for the validity of the act.[92] Exceptional cases are mentioned in canons 1098 and 1099. An incapacitating law is one which renders the person unable to perform an act. Canon 1072 is an example of an incapacitating law,

---

[90] Cf. S. C. S. Officii, 27 ian., 1928—*AAS,* XX (1928), 75; *CLD,* I, 762, 763; Commissio Pontificia ad canones authentice interpretandos, 30 iul., 1934—*AAS,* XXVI (1934), 494; *CLD,* II, 762, 763; S. C. S. Officii, 27 febr. 1937.—"Nova S. Cong. Sancti Officii decisio de significatione vocis 'Acatholicorum.'" *Periodica de Re Canonica, Morali, et Liturgica,* XXVI (1937), 400; *CLD,* II, 531, 532; S. C. S. Officii, 22 mart., 1939—*AAS,* XXXI (1939), 131; *CLD,* II, 547; S. C. S. Officii, 15 ian., 1940—*AAS,* XXXII (1940), 52; *CLD,* II, 534. These documents are cited and analyzed by A. Nace, *The Right to Accuse a Marriage of Invalidity,* The Catholic University of America Canon Law Studies, n. 418 (Washington, D. C.: The Catholic University of America Press, 1961), pp. 94-104.

[91] Nace, *loc. cit.*

[92] Cicognani, *Canon Law,* p. 558; Michiels, *Normae Generales,* I, 343.

for it states that clerics in major orders cannot contract a valid marriage. The distinction between the two kinds of laws lies in the fact that an incapacitating law is a species of invalidating law, at least in regard to its effects.[93] An invalidating law directly affects the act while an incapacitating law indirectly affects the act but directly affects the person who performs the act in denying to him the exercise of a right which he would otherwise enjoy by virtue of the natural law or by the enactment of the positive law. In other words, an incapacitating law prescribes that a person is either absolutely lacking in the ability to place an act or at least he lacks that ability under certain circumstances in such a way that if the act is placed it affects nothing and is considered at law as never to have existed. Canon 11 states the general principle that laws are not to be presumed as invalidating or incapacitating unless these qualities are expressly or equivalently stated.[94]

The general principle of canon 1971, § 1, 1°, states that the spouses are capable of impugning the validity of their marriage under ordinary circumstances; but the second half of that paragraph contains an incapacitating clause inasmuch as it states that the spouses are deprived of this capacity when they are the cause of the impediment. The reasoning is that no person or persons should profit from his or their own misdeeds. In short, the law of canon 1971, § 1, 1°, contains an express statement of procedural incapacity affecting the person directly, and the act of accusation only indirectly, under the circumstances indicated.

It may also be seen that canon 1971, § 1, 1°, restrains a right which is founded on both the natural law right of entering a valid contract and the positive enactments of the Code of Canon Law, to wit, that a right is fortified by an action at law, and that a person may bring an action before an ecclesiastical tribunal, especially in cases of contractual nullity.[95] Such a law must be inter-

---

[93] E. Roelker, *Invalidating Laws* (Paterson, N. J.: St. Anthony Guild Press, 1955), p. 6.

[94] Invalidating laws as found in the Code of Canon Law are analyzed and listed by E. Roelker, *op. cit.*, pp. 136-157.

[95] Canons 1679, 1646 and 1667.

preted strictly according to canon 19, that is, the words used in the law must be understood in their ordinary and proper sense.[96] In other words, canon 1971, § 1, 1°, must be interpreted in such a way that no other elements intervene in its interpretation except those which are necessary for a literal understanding of the canon as it is worded in the Code of Canon Law and as it has been authentically interpreted by the legislator.

---

[96] Cicognani, *Canon Law,* p. 615; Michiels, *Normae Generales Iuris Canonici,* I, 480, 481; M. Shekelton, *Doctrinal Interpretation of Law,* The Catholic University of America Canon Law Studies, n. 345 (Washington, D. C.: The Catholic University of America Press, 1961), p. 91.

## SUMMARY AND CONCLUSIONS

1. The restraint of the exercise of rights in the period before the Code of Canon Law existed in the right of private property as it developed in Roman Law. Before the time of the *Twelve Tables* it is conjectured that the right of private property was originally communal or tribal, later familial, and finally individual. At the time of the *Twelve Tables* individual ownership existed; restrictions also existed in the form of rights of way, etc. In the classical law of Rome these special rights of way were protected by interdicts and in some cases became servitudes. Servitudes were real or personal, and involved rights in the property of others, *iura in re aliena.* It has been conjectured that in post-classical law a "theory of emulative acts" introduced a subjective element into the exercise of rights. It is generally agreed that the "theory of emulative acts" never existed in classical Roman Law (pp. 1-18).

2. Germanic Law was less philosophical and more pragmatic in its character than Roman Law. The German tribes considered the law to be a discovery of the truth rather than the imposition of a command. As regards the right of private property Germanic Law invented the system of the fief and vassalage, which was the substructure of the feudal system. In many instances church lands were given to knights for services to the local lord. Against such abuses the Church protected itself through councils and canonical collections, some of which were spurious and some genuine. These canons spoke of the ownership of church property as a trust, and laid obligations upon its trustees concerning acts of alienation (pp. 19-30).

3. In the texts of Gratian individual rights in property were recognized with corresponding social obligations, especially the support of the needy. As regards the ownership of church property, it was held that the community of the faithful under the Headship of Christ owned the property of the Church. Every Christian had an interest in church property: the laity supported the Church and

provided its goods; the clergy governed the Church and administered its goods; and the poor received their sustenance from the Church and prayed for their benefactors. In this way the rights of property were restrained in the mediaeval Church. In later Canon Law the Church continually restrained the exercise of the rights of trustees of church property as regards its alienation (pp. 31-43).

4. The decrees of the Council of Trent and later legislation, both universal and particular, continued to emphasize the nature of the administrative trust which is the responsibility of the bishops, pastors and major religious superiors. This legislation continued the legal restraint upon the exercise of the right of ownership of church property (pp. 44-46).

5. The source of the law of the Code of Canon Law which treats of the restraint of the exercise of one's rights in canon 19 is found in the Italian Civil Code of 1865 (pp. 47, 48).

6. From the theological point of view the *magisterium* of the Church, Sacred Scripture and the teaching of the Fathers affirm the existence of freedom in man and of a restraint of freedom under certain circumstances (pp. 51-63).

7. From the philosophical point of view the nature of man as a free being and as a social being determines the need for the restraint of his freedom. This necessary restriction is seen as a result of the function of law which has for its purpose the establishment of the common good (pp. 64-74).

8. By baptism a person is incorporated into the Church. The Church is a visible society whose members are bound together both by the profession of the same faith and the sharing of the sacraments under the governance of the Holy Father. Juridical personality arises from baptism by water alone, the profession of the faith, the maintenance of the bond of communion and the lack of excommunication by legitimate authority. Canon Law restrains the rights of those with less than full juridic personality, as well as those who are minors or lack the use of reason. Besides physical persons, moral persons are also affected by the restriction of rights (pp. 75-84).

9. The Code of Canon Law deals as a general rule with ecclesiastical rights which affect only the baptized. Occasionally, however, the Code of Canon Law interprets the divine law, which binds all human beings (pp. 86-87).

10. Persons in their majority generally enjoy the full possession of their rights. Minors are subject to their parents or guardians except in matters which pertain to their state in life. Moral persons are restricted in the exercise of their rights in the law of privileges, in the law of the care of parishes, and in the right of clerical exempt religious in Canon 497, § 2 (pp. 89-97).

11. Among those who possess membership in the Church, but whose rights are nevertheless restrained, are heretics, apostates, schismatics, excommunicates and those under other censures (pp. 97-104).

12. Among those rights which are restrained in the substantive law of the Church are the right of a religious to receive the Holy Eucharist under certain circumstances; the right of clerics to exercise their orders because of irregularities or impediments; the right of persons to marry when they are affected with impediments. A special case is the power of the local ordinary to impose a prohibition to contract a marriage in a particular case, for a just cause, and for a definite time. In like manner the mandatory juridical form of marriage involves a restriction of the exercise of one's rights (pp. 105-118).

13. In procedural law, the law makes provision for the restriction of the exercise of one's rights explicitly in canons 1672-1675, and incidentally in canon 1699, § 3. An application of the restriction of the exercise of one's rights is found also in canon 1971, § 1. 1° (pp. 118-131).

# BIBLIOGRAPHY

## Sources


*Acta Apostolicae Sedis, Commentarium Officiale,* Romae, 1909-1929; Civitate Vaticana, 1929—

*Acta et Decreta Concilii Plenarii Baltimorensis II (1866),* Baltimorae, 1894.

*Acta et Decreta Concilii Plenarii Baltimorensis III (1884),* Baltimorae, 1886.

*Acta et Decreta Sacrorum Conciliorum Recentiorum, Collectio Lacensis,* 7 vols., Friburgi Brisgoviae: Herder, 1870-1892.

*Acta Sanctae Sedis,* 41 vols., Romae, 1865-1908.

Bouscaren, T. Lincoln, *The Canon Law Digest,* 4 vols. and Supplements through 1958, 1959, 1960 and 1961, Milwaukee: Bruce and Company, 1934-1962.

Bruns, H., *Canones Apostolorum et Conciliorum Saeculorum IV-VII,* 2 vols., Berolini, 1839.

*The Church and the Reconstruction of the Modern World,* edited by Terence P. McLoughlin, Garden City, New York: Doubleday and Co., 1957.

*The Church Speaks to the Modern World,* edited by Etienne Gilson, Garden City, New York: Doubleday and Co., 1954.

*Codex Iuris Canonici, Pii X Pontificis Maximi iussu digestus, Benedicti XV auctoritate promulgatus,* Romae: Typis Polyglottis Vaticanis, 1917; reimpressio, 1952.

*Codicis Iuris Canonici Fontes,* cura Emi Petri Gasparri editi, 9 vols., Romae (postea Civitate Vaticana): Typis Polyglottis Vaticanis, 1923-1939. Vols. VII-IX, ed. cura et studio Emi Iustiniani Card. Serédi.

*Corpus Iuris Canonici,* editio Lipsiensis secunda, post Aemilii Ludovici Richteri curas ad librorum manu scriptorum et editionis Romanae fidem recognovit et adnotatione critica instruxit Aemilius Friedburg, 2 vols., Vol. I, *Decretum Magistri Gratiani,* Vol. II, *Decretalium Collectiones Gregorii IX,* Lipsiae: Tauchnitz, 1928.

*Corpus Iuris Civilis,* 3 vols., Vol. I, *Institutiones,* quas recognovit P. Krueger; *Digesta,* quae recognovit T. Mommsen et retractavit P. Krueger, ed. stereotypa 15., Vol. II, *Codex Iustinianus,* quem recognovit et retractavit P. Krueger, ed. Stereotypa 10.; Vol. III, *Novellae Constitutiones,* ed. stereotypa 5., a R. Schoell; opus Schoellii morte interceptum absolvit G. Kroll, Berolini; apud Weidmannos, 1928-1929.

*Corpus Iuris Civilis, suae integritati una cum glossis restitutae,* 4 vols., Vol. I, *Institutiones, Lugduni,* 1549, Vol. II, *Digestum Vetus,* Lugduni, 1550, Vol. III, *Codex,* Lugduni, 1549, *Authenticum, III Libri, Libri Feudorum,* Lugduni, 1550.

*Decretales Gregorii Papae IX,* suae integritati una cum glossis restitutae, 2 vols., Romae, 1582.

*Decretales D. Gregorii Papae IX, suae integritati una cum glossis restitutae, cum privilegio Gregorii XIII, Pont. Max., et Aliorum Principum,* Romae, 1582.

*Decretum Gratiani,* emendatum et notationibus illustratum una cum glossis, 2 vols., Romae, 1582.

Denzinger, Henricus, *Enchiridion Symbolorum definitionum et declarationum de rebus fidei et morum,* quod post Clementem Bannwart et Ioannem B. Umberg denuo edidit Carolus Rahner, editio 31, Herder, Barcinone-Friburgi Brisgoviae-Romae: Herder, 1957.

*Extravagantes Decretales, quae a diversis Romanis Pontificibus Post Sextum emanaverunt, Quarum aliquae Glossis Ioannis Monachi Picardi Cardinalis, aliquae comentariis Guglielmi de Monte Laudano, et Ioannis Francisci de Paomis illustrantur.*

*Fontes Iuris Romani Anteiustiniani,* edd. S. Riccobono, J. Baviera, C. Ferrini, J. Furlani, V. Arrangio-Ruiz, 3 vols., ed. altera, Florentiae: A. G. Barbèra, 1941-1943.

Hardouin, I., *Acta Conciliorum et Epistolae Decretales ac Constitutiones Summorum Pontificum,* 12 vols., Parisiis, 1714-1715.

Hinschius, Paulus, *Decretales Pseudo-Isidorianae,* Leipzig, 1863.

*The Holy Bible,* translated by the Rt. Rev. Msgr. Ronald A. Knox, New York: Sheed and Ward, 1956.

*Italian Civil Code,* Roma, 1865.

Jaffé, Philippus, *Regesta Pontificum Romanorum, ab condita ecclesia ad annum post Christum natum MCXCVIII,* 2. ed., 2 vols., correctam et auctam auspiciis Gulielmi Wattenbach curaverunt F. Kaltenbrunner ad annum 590, P. Ewald ab anno 590 ad annum 882, S. Loewenfeld ab anno 882 ad annum 1198, Lipsiae, 1885-1888.

*Liber Sextus Decretalium D. Bonifatii Papae VIII, Clementis Papae V Constitutiones, Extravagantes tum Viginti D. Ioannis Papae XXII, tum communes, haec omnia cum suis glossis suae integritati restituta et ad exemplar Romanum diligenter recognita,* Taurinae, 1588.

*Liber Sextus Decretalium D. Bonifatii Papae VIII suae integritati cum Clementinis Extravagantibus, earumque Glossis restitutis,* Romae, 1582.

Mansi, Ioannes, *Sacrorum Conciliorum Nova et Amplissima Collectio,* 53 vols. in 60, Vol. I-XXXV, Florentiae, Venetiis, 1758-1798; Vols. XXXVI-LX, Parisiis, 1901-1927, Parisiis, 1901-1927.

*Monumenta Germaniae Historica inde ab anno Christi 500 usque ad annum 1500,* Hannoverae, 1826—; *Leges* in 5 vols., Impensis Bibliopoli Hahniani, 1875-1889.

## Reference Works

Ayrinhac, H. A., *Marriage Legislation in the New Code of Canon Law,* revised and enlarged by P. J. Lydon, New York: Benziger Bros., 1957.

Begin, R., *Natural Law and Positive Law,* The Catholic University of America Canon Law Studies, n. 393, Washington, D. C.: The Catholic University of America Press, 1959.

Bellarmine, St. Robert, *Disputationes de controversiis,* 4 vols., Liber III, *De ecclesia,* Venetiis, 1599.

Bender, Ludovicus, *Philosophia Iuris,* 2. ed., Romae: Officium Libri Catholici, 1955.

Berger, Adolph, *Encyclopedic Dictionary of Roman Law,* Philadelphia: The American Philosophical Society, 1953.

Bernard, Fernand, *First Year of Roman Law,* translated by Charles P. Sherman, Cambridge, 1906.

Beste, Udalricus, *Introductio in Codicem,* 4. ed., Neapoli: M. D'Auria, Pontificius Editor, 1956.

Boich, Henricus, *In Quinque Decretalium Libros Commentaria,* Venetiis, 1576.

Bouscaren, T. L.-Ellis, A. C., *Canon Law, A Text and Commentary,* 3. ed., revised, Milwaukee: Bruce Publishing Co., 1957.

Bowe, T. J., *The Power of Religious Superioresses,* The Catholic University of America Canon Law Studies, n. 228, Washington, D. C.: The Catholic University of America Press, 1946.

Buckland, W. W., and McNair, A. D., *Roman Law and Common Law,* 2. ed., revised by F. H. Lawson, Cambridge: The University Press, 1952.

Cappello, F. M., *Tractatus Canonico-Moralis de Sacramentis,* 5 vols., Vols. I, II, V, 6. ed., Vols. III, IV, 3. ed., Taurini: Marietti, 1949-1953.

*A Catholic Commentary on Holy Scripture,* edited by Dom Bernard Orchard, Edmund F. Sutcliffe, Reginald C. Fuller, Ralph Russell, New York: Thomas Nelson, 1953.

Cicero, Marcus Tullis, *Disputationes Tusculanae,* 5 books in 1 vol., text revised by Thomas Wilson Dougan, Cambridge: The University Press, 1905-1934.

Cicognani, Amleto Giovanni, *Canon Law,* 2. ed., revised, Westminster, 1934.

Claeys-Bouuaert, F. and Simenon, G., *Manuale Juris Canonici,* 3 vols., Vols. I, III, 5. ed.; Vol. II, 3. ed., Gandae et Leodii, 1939.

Clancy, P. M., *The Local Religious Superior,* The Catholic University of America Canon Law Studies, n. 175, Washington, D. C.: The Catholic University of America Press, 1943.

Cleary, Joseph F., *Canonical Limitations on the Alienation of Church Property,* The Catholic University of America Canon Law Studies, n. 100, Washington, D. C.: The Catholic University of America Press, 1936.

Cloran, Owen M., *Previews and Practical Cases, Code of Canon Law, Book Five: Delicts and Penalties,* Milwaukee: Bruce Publishing Co., 1951.

Conran, E., *The Interdict,* The Catholic University of America Canon Law Studies, n. 56, Washington, D. C., 1930.

Conte a Coronata, M., *Institutiones Iuris Canonici,* 4 vols., Vols. I-III, 4. ed., Vol. IV, 3. ed., Taurini: Marietti, 1950-1956.

Creusen, J., and Ellis, A., *Religious Men and Women in Church Law,* 6. ed., Milwaukee: Bruce Publishing Co., 1958.

Cuq, Edouard, *Les Institutiones Juridiques des Romains,* 2 vols., Paris, 1891.

Daly, L. J., *The Political Thought of John Wyclif,* Loyola University Press, Chicago, 1962.

D'Angelo, Sosius, *Ius Digestorum,* 2 vols., Romae, 1927.

D'Avack, P., *Cause di nullita e di divorzio,* 2 vols., 2. ed., Firenze: Casa Editrice del Dott. Carlo Cya., 1952.

De Journel, M. J. Rouet, *Enchiridion Patristicum loci SS. Patrum, doctorum, scriptorum ecclesiasticorum,* editio 21., Friburgi-Brisgoviae: Herder, 1959.

Della Rocca, F., *Canonical Procedure,* translated by John D. Fitzgerald, Milwaukee: Bruce Publishing Co., 1961.

DeSmet, A., *De Sponsalibus et Matrimonio,* 2 vols., 3. ed., Brugis, 1920-1923.

DeWulf, Maurice, *Mediaeval Philosophy,* Cambridge, 1922.

Doheny, W. J., *Canonical Procedure in Matrimonial Cases,* 2 vols., 2. ed., Milwaukee: Bruce Publishing Co., 1948.

Dunnivan, J. P., *Prejudicial Attempts in Pending Litigation,* The Catholic University of America Canon Law Studies, n. 379, Washington, D. C.: The Catholic University of America Press, 1960.

Falco, M., *Introduzione allo studio del Codex Iuris Canonici,* Torino, 1925.

Ford, John C., and Kelly, Gerald, *Contemporary Moral Theology,* Vol. I, *Questions in Fundamental Moral Theology,* Westminster, Md.: Newman Press, 1959.

*Gai Institutiones or Institutes of Roman Law by Gaius,* with a translation by Edward Poste, 4. ed. in 4 books, revised by E. A. Whittuck, Oxford, 1904.

Ganshof, Francois L., *Qu'est-ce que la feodalite?* 2. ed., Neuchatel: Editions de la Baconniere, 1947.

Gasparri, Pietrus, *Tractatus Canonicus de Matrimonio,* 2 vols., nova ed., Typis Polyglottis Vaticanis, 1932.

Grenier, H., *Cursus Philosophiae,* 3 vols., editio altera, Quebec: Le Seminaire de Québec, 1944.

Henricus de Segusio (Hostiensis), *Commentaria in Quinque Libros ad Decretales,* 6 vols. in 4, Venetiis, 1581.

Hickey, J. J., *Irregularities and Simple Impediments,* The Catholic University of America Canon Law Studies, n. 7, Washington, D. C., 1920.

Innocentius IV, *In Quinque Libros Decretalium Commentaria,* Venetiis, 1576.

Jenks, Edward, *Law and Politics in the Middle Ages,* New York, 1898.

Jolowicz, H. F., *Historical Introduction to the Study of Roman Law,* 2. ed., Cambridge: The University Press, 1954.

Lega, M., and Bartoccetti, V., *Commentarius in Iudicia Ecclesiastica iuxta Codicem Iuris Canonici,* 3 vols., ed. a V. Bartoccetti, Romae: Azienda Libraria Cattolica Italiana, 1950.

Livy, *Historiae,* in 13 vols., translated by B. O. Foster, Loeb Classical Library, New York: Putnam's Sons, 1924.

Lot, Ferdinand, *End of the Ancient World and the Beginnings of the Middle Ages,* London, 1931.

MacKenzie, E. F., *The Delict of Heresy,* The Catholic University of America Canon Law Studies, n. 77, Washington, D. C., 1932.

McCloskey, J., *The Subject of Ecclesiastical Law According to Canon 12,* The Catholic University of America Canon Law Studies, n. 165, Washington, D. C.: The Catholic University of America Press, 1943.

McGrath, R. E., *The Local Superior in Non-Exempt Clerical Congregations,* The Catholic University of America Canon Law Studies, n. 351, Washington, D. C.: The Catholic University of America Press, 1954.

Maritain, Jacques, *Scholasticism and Politics,* Garden City, New York: Doubleday and Co., 1960.

Maroto, Philippus, *Institutiones Iuris Canonici ad Normam Novi Codicis,* 2 vols., Vol. I, 3. ed., Matriti, 1921.

Meyer, Hans, *The Philosophy of St. Thomas Aquinas,* translated by Frederic Eckoff, London: Herder, 1944.

Michiels, Gommarus, *Normae Generales Iuris Canonici, Commentarius Libri I Codicis Iuris Canonici,* 2 vols., ed. altera, Parisiis-Tornaci-Romae: Desclée et Socii, 1949.

———, *Principia Generalia de Personis in Ecclesia, Commentarius Libri II Codicis Iuris Canonici. Canones Praeliminares,* ed. altera, Parisiis-Tornaci-Romae: Desclée et Socii, 1955.

Migne, J. P., *Patrologiae Cursus Completus, Series Graeca,* 161 vols., Parisiis, 1857-1866.

———, *Patrologiae Cursus Completus, Series Latina,* 221 vols., Parisiis, 1844-1855.

Mortimer, R. C., *Western Canon Law,* Los Angeles: University of California Press, 1953.

Muirhead, James, *Historical Introduction to the Private Law of Rome,* 3. ed., revised by Alexander Grant, London, 1916.

Nace, Arthur, *The Right to Accuse a Marriage of Invalidity,* The Catholic University of America Canon Law Studies, n. 418, Washington, D. C.: The Catholic University of America Press, 1961.

Noval, J., *Commentarium in Codicem Iuris Canonici,* Liber IV, *De Processibus,* Pars I, *De Iudiciis,* Romae, 1920.

O'Donnell, Cletus, *The Marriage of Minors,* The Catholic University of America Canon Law Studies, n. 221, Washington, D. C.: The Catholic University of America Press, 1945.

Ottaviani, Alaphridus, *Institutiones Iuris Publici Ecclesiastici,* 2 vols., Vol. I, *Ecclesiae Constitutio Socialis et Potestas,* 4. ed., Romae: Typis Polyglottis Vaticanis, 1958.

Petrovits, J. J., *The New Church Law on Matrimony,* The Catholic University of America Canon Law Studies, n. 6, Philadelphia, 1921.

Prat, Ferdinand, *The Theology of St. Paul,* translated by John L. Stoddard, 2 vols., Westminster, Md., 1926.

Rainer, E. G., *Suspension of Clerics,* The Catholic University of America Canon Law Studies, n. 111, Washington, D. C., 1937.

Regatillo, Eduardo, *Institutiones Iuris Canonici,* 2 vols., 5. ed., Santander: Sal Terrae, 1956.

Ricciotti, Giuseppe, *Paul the Apostle,* translated by Alba I. Zizzamia, Milwaukee: Bruce Publishing Co., 1953.

Roberti, F., *De Processibus,* 4. ed., Romae: Apud Custodiam Librariam Pontificii Instituti Utriusque Iuris, 1956.

Roby, Henry John, *Roman Private Law in the Times of Cicero and the Antonines,* 2 vols., Cambridge, 1902.

Rodimer, F. J., *The Canonical Effects of Infamy of Fact,* The Catholic University of America Canon Law Studies, n. 353, Washington, D. C.: The Catholic University of America Press, 1954.

Roelker, Edward, *Invalidating Laws,* Paterson, N. J.: St. Anthony Guild Press, 1955.

———, *Principles of Privileges According to the Code of Canon Law,* The Catholic University of America Canon Law Studies, n. 35, Washington, D. C., 1926.

Rzadkiewicz, Arnold, *The Philosophical Bases of Human Liberty according to St. Thomas Aquinas,* The Catholic University of America, Philosophical Series, n. 105, Washington, D. C.: The Catholic University of America Press, 1949.

*Saint Thomas Aquinas: Philosophical Texts,* edited by Thomas Gilbey, New York: Oxford University Press, 1951.

Saint Thomas Aquinas, *Summa Theologica,* translated by the Fathers of the English Dominican Province, 3 vols., New York: Benziger Brothers, 1947.

*Sancti Thomae Aquinatis Omnia Opera,* 25 vols., New York: Musurgia Press, 1948.

*De Regimine Principum ad Regem Cypri,*
*De Veritate,*
*In Libros Ethicorum,*
*In Libros Politicorum,*
*In Quatuor Libros Sententiarum,*
*Summa Contra Gentiles,*
*Summa Theologica.*

Schaefer, T., *De Religiosis,* 3. ed., Romae: Herder, 1940.

Schulz, Fritz, *Classical Roman Law,* Oxford: The University Press, 1954.

———, *Principles of Roman Law,* Oxford: The University Press, 1936.

Shekleton, Matthew M., *Doctrinal Interpretation of Law,* The Catholic University of America Canon Law Studies, n. 345, Washington, D. C.: The Catholic University of America Press, 1961.

Suarez, Franciscus, *Tractatus de Legibus,* Antwerpiae, 1631.

Tatarczuk, V. A., *Infamy of Law,* The Catholic University of America Canon Law Studies, n. 357, Washington, D. C.: The Catholic University of America Press, 1954.

Thaner, F., *Anselmi Luccensis collectio canonum una cum collectione minore,* 2 vols., Innsbruck, 1906-1915.

Tierney, Brian, *Mediaeval Poor Law,* Berkeley and Los Angeles: University of California Press, 1959.

Tierney, William J., *Authorized Ecclesiastical Acts,* The Catholic University of America Canon Law Studies, n. 414, Washington, D. C.: The Catholic University of America Press, 1961.

Van Hove, Alphonsus, *Commentarium Lovaniense in Codicem Iuris Canonici,* 1 vol. in 5 tomes, Tome I, *Prolegomena,* 2. ed., 1945; Tome II, *De Legibus Ecclesiasticis,* Romae: Dessain, 1930.

Van Ommeren, William M., *Mental Illness Affecting Matrimonial Consent,* The Catholic University of America Canon Law Studies, n. 415, Washington, D. C.: The Catholic University of America Press, 1961.

Varro, L. L., *De Lingua Latina,* translated by Roland G. Kent, New York, 1924.

Vermeersch, A., *Epitome Iuris Canonici,* 3 vols., 3. ed., Mechliniae-Romae, 1927.

———, *Theologia Moralis,* 3 vols., 4. ed., Romae-Brugis, 1926.

Vermeersch, A., and Creusen, J., *Epitome Iuris Canonici,* 3 vols., 7. ed., Mechliniae-Romae: Dessain, 1949-1956.

Wernz, F., and Vidal, P., *Ius Canonicum ad Normam Codicis Exactum,* 7 vols. in 8, Vol. II, 3. ed., Romae: Apud Aedes Universitatis Gregorianae, 1943.

———, *Ius Canonicum ad Normam Codicis Exactum,* 7 vols. in 8, Tomus VI, *De Processibus,* ed. altera, a F. Cappello, recognita, Romae: Apud Aedes Universitatis Gregorianae, 1949.

Vogelpohl, H. J., *The Simple Impediment to Holy Orders,* The Catholic University of America Canon Law Studies, n. 224, Washington, D. C.: The Catholic University of America Press, 1945.

Waterhouse, J. M., *The Power of the Local Ordinary to Impose a Matrimonial Ban,* The Catholic University of America Canon Law Studies, n. 317, Washington, D. C.: The Catholic University of America Press, 1952.

Westrup, C. W., *Introduction to Early Roman Law,* Comparative Sociological Studies, 5 vols. in 3, London: Oxford University Press, 1934-1950.

## Articles

Anon., "Nova S. Cong. Sancti Oficii decisio de significatione vocis 'Acatholicorum,'" *Periodica,* XXVI (1937), 400.

Barry, John C., "The Tridentine Form of Marriage: Is the Law Unreasonable?" *The Jurist,* XX (1960), 159-178.

Ciprotti, P., "Personalità e Battesimo nel diritto della Chiesa," *Il Diritto Ecclesiastico,* LIII (1942), 273-276.

DeKoninck, Charles, "In Defense of Saint Thomas," *Laval Théologique et Philosophique,* I (1945), 9-109.

Fabregas, P. M., "Aliqua de natura boni communis," *Periodica,* XLII (1953), 246-262.

Gismondi, P., "Gli acatholici nel diritto della Chiesa," *Ephemerides Iuris Canonici,* II (1946), 224-249; III (1947), 20-55; IV (1948), 55-68.

Lobo, A., "Tiene la Acciòn Catolica personalidad moral eclesiastica?" *Revista Española de Derecho Canonico,* VII (1952), 289-312.

Onçlin, W., "Considerationes de iurium subiectivorum in Ecclesia fundamento ac natura," *Ephemerides Iuris Canonici,* VIII (1952), 9-23.

Piontek, C., "De Acephalis in Iure Canonico," *Ius Pontificium,* XIV (1934), 194-215; 284-294; XV (1935), 56-63; 202-208; XVII (1937), 64-82.

### Dictionaries and Encyclopedias

*Dictionary of the Bible,* edited by James Hastings, 4 vols., New York, 1900.

*Dictionnaire de la Bible,* ed. par F. Vigouroux, 5 vols., Paris, 1912.

*Encyclopedia of the Social Sciences,* edited by Edwin R. A. Seligman, 15 vols., New York: The Macmillan Company, 1935.

*Oxford Classical Dictionary,* edited by M. Cory, A. D. Nock, J. D. Dennison, J. Wight Duff, W. D. Ross, H. H. Scullard, London: Oxford University Press, 1949.

### Periodicals

*Ephemerides Iuris Canonici,* Romae, 1945—

*Il Diritto Ecclesiastico,* Romae, 1890—

*Jus Pontificium,* Romae, 1921-1940.

*Jurist, The,* Washington, D. C., 1941—

*Laval Théologique et Philosophique,* Québec, 1945—

*Periodica de Re Canonica et Morali,* Brugis, 1920-1927; *Periodica de Re Morali, Canonica, Liturgica,* Brugis, 1927-1936, et Romae, 1937—

*Revista Española de Derecho Canonico,* Madrid, 1946—

## BIOGRAPHICAL NOTE

John C. Calhoun was born on May 8, 1932, in Jersey City, New Jersey. He received his elementary education at St. Teresa of Avila Grammar School, Brooklyn, New York. He was graduated from Cathedral College High School in June, 1950, and from Cathedral College in 1952. In September of that year he entered the Diocesan Seminary of the Immaculate Conception, Huntington, New York, from which he received the Bachelor of Arts degree in June, 1954. Upon completion of his theological studies at the Seminary of the Immaculate Conception he was awarded the degree of Bachelor of Sacred Theology from The Catholic University of America in 1958. He was ordained to the Holy Priesthood on May 31, 1958, by His Excellency, the Most Reverend Bryan J. McEntegart, D.D., LL.D., Bishop of Brooklyn. He was assigned to St. Augustine Parish, Brooklyn, until September, 1960, when he entered the School of Canon Law of The Catholic University of America, Washington, D. C. He received the Baccalaureate degree in Canon Law in June, 1961. He received the degree of Licentiate in Canon Law in 1962.

## INDEX

## CANON LAW STUDIES*

430. Bonner, Rev. Dismas W., O.F.M., B.A., J.C.L., Extern sisters in monasteries of nuns.
431. Bowen, Rev. Henry G., A.B., Ph.B., S.T.L., J.C.L., The juridic authority of the Church over the non-baptized. (Microfilm)
432. Calhoun, Rev. John C., B.A., S.T.B., J.C.L., The restraint of the exercise of one's rights.
433. Goeke, Rev. John W., B.A., J.C.L., The laws of the state of Kentucky affecting Church property. (Microfilm)
434. Swierzowski, Rev. Stanislaus J., S.T.L., M.S., J.C.L., Catholic parties in civil separation and divorce cases.
435. Voegtle, Brother Leonard A., F.M.S., B.A., M.A., J.C.L., Canonical reasons for the rejection of candidates to final vows. (Microfilm)

---

*For a complete list of the available numbers of this series apply to the Catholic University of America Press, 620 Michigan Avenue, N.E., Washington 17, D. C., for a general catalogue.

www.ingramcontent.com/pod-product-compliance
Lightning Source LLC
LaVergne TN
LVHW050221080826
844660LV00012B/451

* 9 7 8 0 8 1 3 2 2 6 7 6 7 *